# Teach All About It

100 Down-To-Earth Tips For Making The Most Out Of Your Classroom

By H A Billinghurst

Content © Copyright H A Billinghurst, 2018
Cover Illustration Copyright © Soni Speight, 2018 - htttps://www.sonispeight.com


The right of Holly Billinghurst to be identified as the author of this work has been asserted by her in accordance with the Copyright, Designs and Patents act 1988

Every reasonable effort has been made to trace copyright holder of material reproduced in this book, but if any have been inadvertently overlooked the publishers would be glad to hear from them. For legal purposes the acknowledgements throughout constitute an extension of this copyright page.

All Rights Reserved. No part of this book may be reproduced, stored in a retrieval system, or transmitted at any time or by any means mechanical, electronic, photocopying, recording, or otherwise, without the prior written permission of the publisher.

No responsibility for loss caused to any individual or organization acting on or refraining from action as a result of the material in this publication can be accepted by the publisher or author.

A CIP record of this book is available from the British Library

First printed December 2018

ISBN: *978-1-78926-970-3*

Published by Independent Publishing Network

To find out more about Holly Billinghurst and this book visit
www.TeachAllAboutIT.school

# Foreword

I wasn't meant to be writing a book. I had a clear plan for the summer that involved outdoors and swimming in the sun. Somehow, that all vanished when I started developing #TeacherTips on Twitter which led to an idea (never good) that actually, I would have really appreciated someone giving me some clear tips about how to really handle a classroom.

Having had quite a varied career including social work, youth offending (officer, not offender!), and software development, teaching keeps pulling me back. In fact, after a decade in teaching I'm now juggling classroom teaching, online tutoring, and a number of side hustles in writing (*bingo! First terrible teaching buzzword in the bag – I promise to avoid these as much as possible*). But, if you're considering teaching, tutoring, or any combination involving inspiring young people then hold onto your hat because this magic carpet ride of a career really will show you the world. Sometimes the world can actually be quite terrifying and make you question every choice that you ever made. And you know what? It's ok to feel worried and wonder what went wrong. If anything, worrying about your class at 3am means that you care and have the fire in your belly to make a change.

The ideas collected here are the cumulation of over a decade in the classroom and working with students individually as a tutor. For those of you who have never considered tutoring, I cannot recommend it highly enough as a way to engage with the struggles our students face as individuals.

Not every idea has been developed solely from my classroom, and I have to thank the volumes of teachers who give up their evenings to attend my monthly webinars and weekly Q&A online. Your questions have inspired me to think deeper about the way we present ourselves as teachers and the importance of metacognition.

Hopefully, some of these ideas will bring a little bit of joy to your classroom and make sense of why the kid at the front just launched a fidget spinner at your projector.

As teachers and tutors, we are so many things to so many people and this can feel overwhelming much of the time. We spend much of our time acting like swans – gracefully gliding through our classrooms with the appearance of an adult who has everything together, while actually underneath we're paddling for all we're worth.

Some swans even fool their colleagues into not seeing the paddling feet – so if you're aa PGCE student, an NQT, or even a seasoned teacher who is comparing yourself to a swan, stop it. All the time you're paddling, you're above the water. **You've got this.**

# Acknowledgements

Those who have supported my endless, self-indulgent hours of writing deserve not only an acknowledgement, but possibly a medal for their patience and delivery of cups of tea. Tom, my husband, muse, and constant source of amusement has facilitated this book by taking over the job of both parents as I swore gently at the laptop whilst writers block would only be eased by copious volumes of caffeine. The sleep deprivation caused by my consistent flashes of 2am inspiration resulting in furious laptop tapping were nothing short of torturous.

Catherine and Shell who have put up with me harassing them via instant messaging for months and bouncing ideas off of them, and in the case of Flapjack learning, wholeheartedly taking a wine driven conversation and turning it into educational theory.

Finally, my editor Catharine, without whom this book would be the late night rantings of an overtired teacher. Your patience and good humour allowed me to finish what started out as an extended blog post. You've earned every penny and I can't wait to work with you on the next instalment!

## Table of Contents

| | |
|---|---|
| FOREWORD | 3 |
| ACKNOWLEDGEMENTS | 5 |
| PRECIPITATION IS ANYTHING THAT FALLS FROM THE SKY THAT ISN'T BIRD SHIT | 7 |
| YOU GOTTA' LOVE 'EM | 13 |
| I DO NOT NEGOTIATE WITH TERRORISTS | 23 |
| YOU'VE GOT THE MUSIC IN YOU | 30 |
| WORK FOR IDLE HANDS | 40 |
| YOU ARE HERE | 47 |
| 5,4,3,2,1... BLAST OFF! | 56 |
| FRANKLY MY DEAR... | 65 |
| YOU CAN COUNT ON ME, I'M A MATHS TEACHER | 74 |
| THE BIG BAD I SAID NO! | 83 |
| REFERENCES | 91 |

# Precipitation is Anything That Falls From The Sky That Isn't Bird Shit

This was a direct quote from my GCSE Geography Teacher and 20+ years later I can still remember it word for word. Kudos to you Mr Foxwell. Despite not really wanting to study the subject, I look back on his lessons fondly because he added an element of humour that I have tried to embed into my own lessons.

Why? Because it sparks something in your brain. Literally in fact – laughing produces endorphins which in turn reduce anxiety and pain and create positive micro-moments that encourage whatever we are doing at the time to move into long term memory.

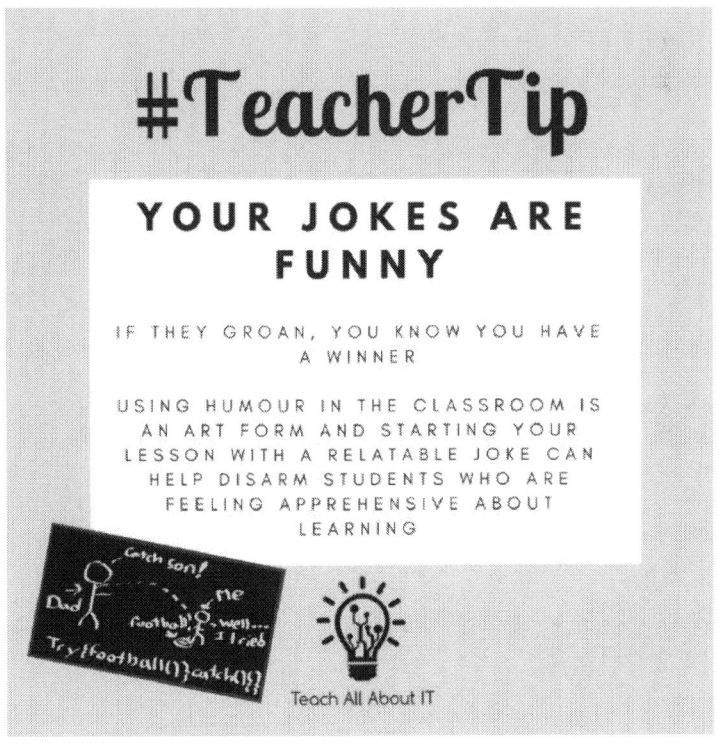

In her 2016 article, "Start Thinking of Micro Learning Moments Now", Karla Gutierrez looks at the value of harnessing the micro moment culture which has evolved from our digital world. Students are no different to adults in their desire to grasp the basics fast.

She defines micro-moments as: "intent-rich moments when a person turns to a device to act on a need"

**Humour** creates a powerful connection between what your students need to know and what they want to know. Clearly, I'm not saying that you should instantly turn into a stand-up comedian in your classroom, but the things that you do to reduce stress and make the room a more pleasant environment will inevitably have a positive impact on the progress that your students make.

Imagine it from an adult perspective – what makes you pay attention in a staff meeting? Is it the serious on-screen presentation (known by so many as 'death by PowerPoint') with more bullet points than you have had hot dinners? Or is it that one engaging presenter who put up a visual slide and oozes enthusiasm and good humour? If we're honest (and teachers make the *very* worst students), we pay attention if we're entertained.

So how do we harness the power of entertainment, whilst still running a tight ship? Learning from successful online practices may well be the key to creating micro moments that ring true for our students. These top ten ideas may help you get started in your own classroom:

### 1. Start with a meme

Set the scene for your lesson by displaying a relevant meme on the board either introducing the topic, or with an 'in joke' that they'll only get once the topic is explained. I use this quite a bit on my Instagram profile to engage learners into some sneaky revision (and students aren't *always* horrified when you're funny).

If you opt to show a meme that they may not instantly understand, display it again at the end of the lesson or section and all of a sudden you have created an 'in joke' with your class, and as a result, forged positive relationships.

As much as we have evolved, we retain a desire to be part of a tribe. Form your tribe with collectively shared knowledge.

## 2. Bring in a puppet

The day I arrived in my Year 10 class with a puppet has stuck in my memory as a risk that paid off. After some research online, I created a Muppet style IT teacher who arrived in my online safety class to explain the (previously dry) concepts to them.

I was initially met with a sea of horrified teenage faces as I had a full conversation with Mr Iteration about how his account had been hacked due to his poor use of the three factors of cyber security. I finished the lesson questioning my own sanity and whether was the single most awkward lesson I would ever teach. The next lesson, every student asked where Mr Iteration was and when he's be teaching them again.

The puppet made a few more appearances as a treat and spent the rest of the academic year as our mascot. And remains a constant reminder to me that you can't gauge a teenager's level of interest through external factors alone!

## 3. Add some cosplay

I'm not suggesting that you arrive in your classroom dressed fully as Jane Austen (although, far be it from me to judge if you do!). However, adding an element of recognisable costume can be used as an ice-breaker or visual learning element to help students remember a particular topic.

A number of my lessons on sorting algorithms have been accompanied by me (and the students) wearing a rather famous wizarding hat. Even something as simple as a badge with a book quote can spark a conversation with a student.

Not only does it create a visual element to aid learning, but it shows students that you are not above finding the fun in the subject.

## 4. Add some music

When I first started teaching in secondary schools, my calm and controlled morning class was often shattered by the terrifically cheesy music of our deputy head. Her class arrived in her room beaming as they opened the door to Mama Mia, or We Will Rock You and a cheery greeting from the loudest voice I have ever encountered (I can still hear her cheery greetings to both staff and students of "Good morning darling!").

It was a bit of a shock as an introvert, but over the course of a term I noticed that her students weren't dogged by the tiredness of many others. Undoubtedly, 90% of this was down to her infectious enthusiasm, but a large part of that was spring boarded by the emotional response to the music that greeted them at the start. No matter who entered that room, they were left in no doubt that they needed to hit the ground running.

So kids, now you know that you can blame Miss T for that assault on your ears each morning! Even if you've never met her, the ripples live on.

## 5. Write a joke

This is a bit misleading as a title. Rather than you as the teacher writing the joke, greet them with something terrible - a true 'groaner' – then challenge them to write something better, but still linked to the topic of the lesson. At the end, the class must vote for the best joke of the lesson which is proudly displayed until the next lesson.

As a method of getting students to think deeply about a topic, and analyse its meaning without realising, this is a true winner.

## 6. Create a on offline video

Learning from some of the most popular YouTubers can be of value here. Even when they are just talking to the screen, they add overlays of the main points, or have an image or icon pop up to make a point stick out.

Create an offline version of this by having pre-made signs that you hold up in class (*making a set of these that can be re-used and having placed them strategically around the classroom before the lesson, you frantically racing the room around to hold them up will create a reason for your students to pay attention to what you are saying. It will also promote movement around the classroom taking away the ability to hide at the back of the class*).

Scan the QR code above to download a template to create your own call out signs.

## 7. Engage the cuteness

There is a saying that 90% of the internet is cute cat videos, and it's possible that this is not far wrong. But what is the appeal with so many cats knocking things off of surfaces and jumping into cardboard boxes? Adding these cute images to the introductory slides or starter tasks could actually have an impact on more than just the atmosphere of the class.

In their 2012 study, The Power of Kawaii, Nittono, Fukushima, Yano, & Moriya looked at the effects of viewing cute images on subsequent task performance. Their study concentrated on the impact on memory and concentration and produced some unexpected results. Following the study, it was identified that viewing images largely considered to be 'cute' such as kittens and puppies increased the level of focus and task accuracy of the subjects. Conversely, the time the subjects took to complete a task was slowed, largely because they were more inclined to focus for longer and engage with the tasks in a more methodical way.

## 8. Head down a rabbit hole

How often have you rewarded yourself with a few minutes on YouTube only to find yourself somehow watching "ten reasons your toes are important" or something equally odd? With a very simple hook, we often find ourselves unwittingly clicking on the next thing in search of another hit of entertainment.

Very rarely is the next video (or article) actually the next in a series, but instead something that allows us to veer off on a tangent whilst remaining on the site. Harnessing this powerful social engineering technique in the classroom requires an initial hook by you to engage your students and then a range of resources that allow them to follow a tangent of learning where they investigate a chain of topics.

This can then be tied together with a set of 60 second presentations, or speed learning from each table either at the end of the lesson, or even better at the start of the next lesson with a home learning task to prepare.

## 9. Other things you might like...

Underestimating the power of advertising may be a missed opportunity in teaching. Our students have grown up surrounded by adverts, online influencers, and careful algorithms that encourages them to part with their cash.

It is estimated that a whopping 35% of Amazon's revenue comes from their recommendation engine. So what if we harnessed this as teachers?

After a piece of positive feedback, why not back up that micro moment with a suggestion for further reading or an interesting video that's linked. Having a set of photocopied or scanned short articles could help make this task easier for you, and enable you to differentiate and make your feedback personal.

Out of a class of 30, if 10 students buy into your recommendations you've tapped into a gold mine of independent learning.

## 10. Harness the USP

Whilst we discuss the topic of marketing in the classroom, what is *your* Unique Selling Point? I don't mean your subject, but you specifically. Why do students look forward to your lessons? (If you're feeling a bit flat & don't think that they do, change this to 'what aspect of your lessons do you want students to look forward to?'). More specifically, what do you do that creates a positive impact for your students?

For some this may be creativity in the activities, for others this may be the links to employment that make a subject more tangible. But no matter whether you are the teacher that introduces SURDS with a rap, or produces understandable Geography revision sheets for every lesson, harnessing your strengths to engage students allows you to hone the 'rinse and repeat' area that will make the biggest impact on your students.

For me, it's enthusiasm and the relationship I have with them as individuals. I have honed a persona of being incredibly positive about even the driest of dry topics. This is mainly down to using the *fake it 'til you make it* technique – no matter how grumpy I may feel, one large cup of coffee and a deep breath later, I charge into my classroom announcing the topic in my standard over-enthusiastic manner. After a few minutes, I manage to convince even myself that this is going to be great, and off we go!

## You Gotta' Love 'Em

The title of this second chapter is another quote, this time from an old head teacher of a particularly posh independent school (this made me laugh as the grammar was terrible!) whilst he was addressing the staff at the start of the academic year.

Working with kids is hard. Facilitating the success of 200+ kids in your subject is really hard. Making each one feel like you are invested in them as a person is nigh on Herculean, but not impossible.

When my children were little, rather than a favourite teacher they had a favourite adult. Mary, the lady who ran the school office. At the end of each day, she would say goodbye to each and every one of them personally. By name.

Every day, each child left knowing that they were not invisible and the same was true of the parents. After a career spanning 40 years at the same school, Mary retired to a fanfare from parents who were once the children she said goodbye to, and were now sending their children there because of her.

No-one expects you to be Mary, but there are things that you can do as an educator to let kids know that you see them.

One of the most overwhelming things that I found as a brand new teacher, and again each time I moved schools was creating an individual bond with a vast number of students, but over the years I have developed some tricks that allow me to do this much quicker without the students realising that I'm cheating!

I use IT to help me along the way, using websites such as Quizlet (https://quizlet.com) where students create their own profiles but access my resources to help them learn. When setting up their profiles, they're encouraged to add a selfie as their profile picture. Not only does this give them more ownership of their account, but every time I see their work its shown alongside a photo of them helping to put a name to a face and cement their name in my memory!

Offline alternatives such as adding photos to folders / books are just as powerful. By seeing their photo each time you mark work, you're creating your own micro learning moment alongside that student.

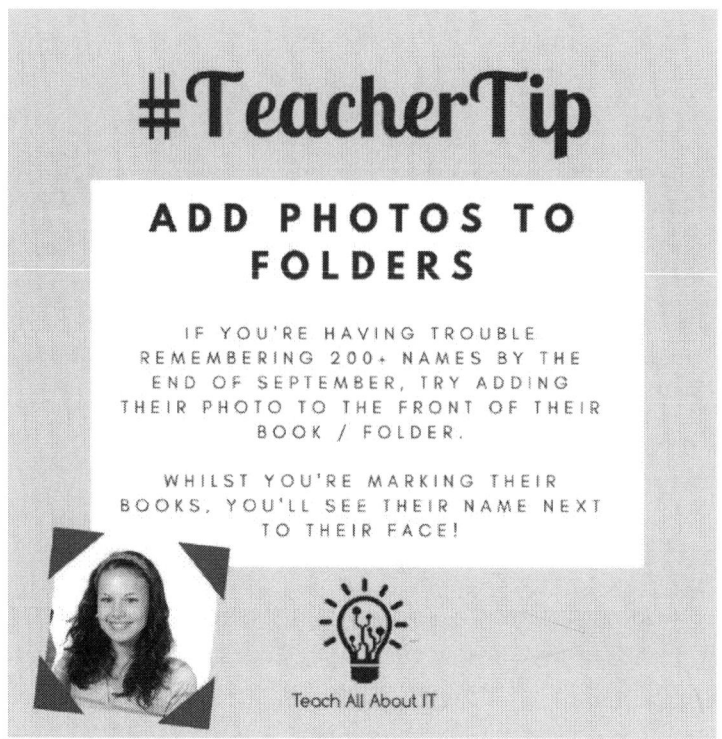

## See them!

That sounds so obvious, but so often we focus on our students who aren't on task, or who out-perform the group. LPA & HPA[1] students are important but those MPA[2] students often fly under the radar until disaster strikes. Too often this is too late – use strategies to make sure that you've spoken personally to each of your students at least once every other lesson (or more if you have smaller classes).

It's tough enough imparting knowledge, but here are a few tips of how to create impactful relationships with your students without losing that much needed sleep at the beginning of the school year (or in fact all year round…).

---

[1] LPA – Low Prior Attainment / HPA – High Prior Attainment

[2] MPA – Middle Prior Attainment

## 11. Add some book stickers

This is a winner no matter what year group you work with. Maybe surprisingly, even 'cool' teenagers like to earn reward stickers. Each time you take books in for marking, try adding a sticker with a single positive comment on the front of their book. Having stickers on display becomes the academic equivalent of Pokémon, creating an instant praise point for others who see them and developing a drive to collect more – gotta catch em all!

Buying packs of several hundred stickers online will often cost just a few pounds, but the positive comments received from both parents and students at the first parents evening when I tried this with a year 9 class convinced me that it was a winner.

Not every student earnt a sticker, but I looked for valid reasons for as many as I could. Interestingly, it was the obvious positive comments that made the difference – high expectations often mean that we overlook those who are meeting expectations, but a sticker that says "your presentation was great", or "I liked how you went back to solve that problem" lets them know that you *do* notice. Even the students who began the year with 'cool' credibility to maintain started to scour the fronts of their books for a new sticker after they were marked (especially midway through the year after they collected too many to count!).

## 12. Create a lolly stick name prompter

If you find that you forget who you've spoken to, or are worried that you'll miss someone out – write down a tally of feedback, create "verbal feedback" stamps or book stickers, or simply use a lolly stick tally where you pick up the stick from their desk after you've spoken to them.

A quick trip through Amazon could net you 50 lolly sticks for under £3, making this a cost effective way to implement a whole host of resources.[3]

With their names on the sticks, you'll seem like a memory master!

---

[3] Find Lolly Sticks: https://amzn.to/2O9CWvT

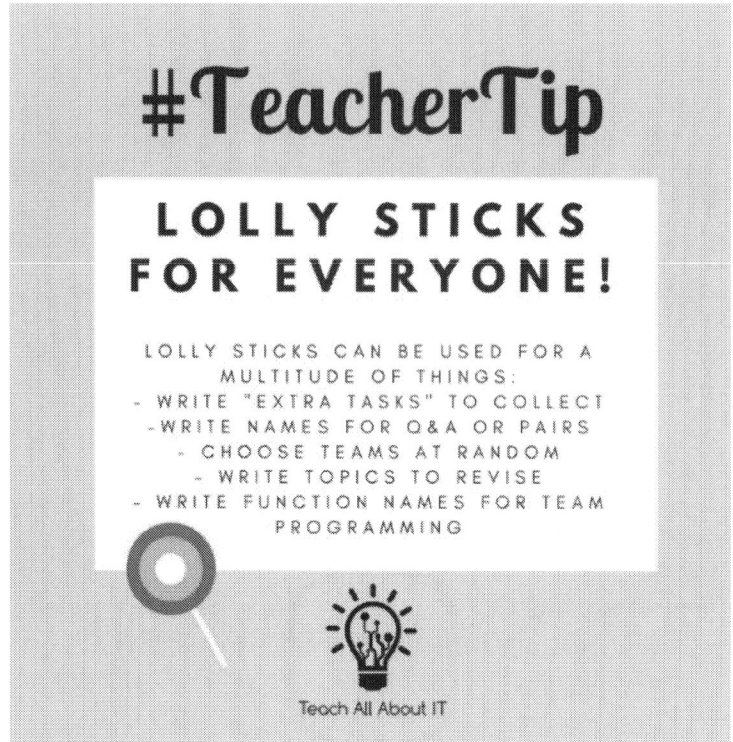

## 13. Harness the power of 'Yet'

There is no sentence uttered by a student that prickles the back of my neck than "I don't get it", especially when it's said loudly before even reading the instructions for a task.

However, this is my problem, not the student's.

I can hear you asking already if it's because the instructions aren't clear enough, or is it in the wrong font?, or even is it just too hard?

It's likely none of these, but a psychological self-protection method that we all use. When pushed out of our comfort zone, not trying means not failing. Failure is a terrifically misunderstood term in our educational society – getting something wrong, is **not** failing. It's learning.

As a way to combat both my own issues with the phrase, and change the way my students think about a task I add the word "…yet!" as I cheerfully glide past them.

*Think about how that changes a sentence:*

I can't read.... **Yet!**

I don't like maths... **Yet!**

I don't know how to get them to behave... **Yet!**

 I first came across this idea whilst watching a Ted Talk by Carol Dweck (*scan the QR code to watch the video*). I'm a little sceptical about the way that 'Growth Mindset' has been implemented in some schools, but the idea that we can use something simple to improve the self-worth of students and teachers? That's something I'll wave a banner for.

It doesn't just work with students either. When you are having the worst day: when your classes are all disruptive, your lesson plans have gone to pot, and to top it all off you've just dropped your marking all over the floor, it would be so easy to just shout "I don't know how to cope with this.... YET!"

The yet is going to allow you space to stop and think about how you can turn it around.

*What have I done before that I could use again to help?*

*If I just try something and it fails on its bum, realistically what is the worst that would happen?*

*Who, or what can I use to help me?*

And bingo! You've turned a horrible feeling into a challenge.

Of course, this isn't going to work immediately and many of your students are going to roll their eyes almost audibly at you.

However, little by little and using adaptations of the questions above, you can show them how to look at the tough stuff as a challenge. As a starting point, ask them to point to evidence of when you told them off for trying & getting something wrong. *"I haven't? Then why would I start now?"*

## 14. Thank them

That seems quite obvious doesn't it? But it's not the obvious thank you to students who help at an open evening, or tidy up after a class. When a student hands in their work - "thank you", when they hold a door open (and they do, more than we notice) – "thank you", when they pick up another student's pen and you see it – "thank you". Young people have had a bad rap for centuries for being impolite and poorly behaved, when in fact it's just easier to notice the negative.

Going back to the micro-moments in chapter one, every time you thank a student for something small, you're creating a positive interaction.

Taking this a step further one year, I decided to try an experiment. Before the start of the academic year, I bought a bulk set of birthday cards with enough for each student in my form. I wrote them a simple card from "Mrs Billinghurst & your friends in 11HAB" and put them into a folder in date order. As each birthday rolled around, these card were left on their desks (either on the day, or the Friday before). Without exception, they mentioned those cards as a positive moment in their leaving book. Did it directly enhance their learning? Probably not. But did it have a knock on effect to how positively they undertook learning for the rest of the day? I'd argue that it did.

## 15. Apologise

Intrinsically linked to the advice above is admitting when you're wrong. We are not infallible and it's not just ok to admit when we get things wrong, but shows our students that we are also embracing the power of **Yet**.

Talking to parents and teachers recently was a real eye-opener on how much respect teachers gain from acknowledging their mistakes and learning from their students. One comment in particular highlighted the distinction:

*"Seth's teacher tried to teach him wrong maths the other day. He politely corrected her but she persisted in saying she was correct. He said 'I just wrote down the right thing and not the wrong thing she said. I did try to explain it to her to help her understand'."* – Sarah Lou

As a Computer Science teacher and tutor, I have extensive experience of my students outshining me and finding errors in my code. It's par of the course with my topic, and in fact the day that a student exceeds my own understanding of a programming topic is the day that I'm doing my job well. With a subject in a constant state of evolution, I've been forced to accept that my knowledge is finite and as long as it's done politely like the young man above, learning from my students is just as beneficial for me! Don't be afraid to admit when you get something wrong – ultimately, your class will respect you more for it.

## 16. Beat the teacher (not literally)

Once you feel comfortable with your students challenging you, a game of 'beat the teacher' rarely fails to engage the competitive streak in our students.

It's useful to note that I said *"once you feel comfortable"*. In our PGCE or NQT year, we are constantly challenging our boundaries purely with pedagogy and have rarely reached a stage where we are fully confident in our own subject knowledge, especially if we have gone into teaching direct from university. Just like we would do for our students, introduce this slowly to build up your confidence.

There are a number of ways to use this concept of challenging the teacher in a positive way in a classroom, or even one to one in tuition:

- Question / Answer race (*Can you answer faster than the teacher?*)
- Exam question relays (*Can your team overload the teacher with marking?*)
- Spot the mistake (*Can you find the teacher's mistakes? – on the board or on paper*)
- Mark the answer (*Can you correct the teacher's work?*)
- Improve the answer (*Can you change the teacher's answer for even more marks?*)

## 17. Get retro with fuzzy felt

When I needed my year 11 class to remember the internal parts of a computer, I was acutely aware that I didn't have access to a set of machines that they could pull apart. Instead, over a weekend I went into the local craft shop and bought some thick card and a pack of felt sheets in multiple colours.

An low, a set of motherboard fuzzy felts were born.

For the students in my class, what this meant was that I was not *just* interested in them knowing facts, but took their stress levels into consideration by including an activity that they perceived as fun and a world away from exam question practice. Whilst we were studying and revising a topic that covered an alarming number of key terms, we found a way to tap into the feel good factor of adding 'play' to our learning.

> *"Tell me and I forget, teach me and I may remember, involve me and I learn" – Benjamin Franklin*

This concept works equally well with any creative material that isn't permanent, allowing mistakes to be tidied away – play dough is particularly good for creating visual representations, or even spelling key terms. This is the same idea as using mini-whiteboards, just a little more creative!

## 18. Score a touchdown!

Anyone that knows me will be aware of my love of American Football, and using my personal interest in this has created some 'interesting' encouragement techniques. One of which includes setting up grade charts in the form of a football field…

Students' avatars start off at the 50 yard line (centre) then move at equal intervals towards their personal End Zone linked to a target grade to score a touchdown. Adding student photos to players bodies added an extra touch of humour to the whole activity.

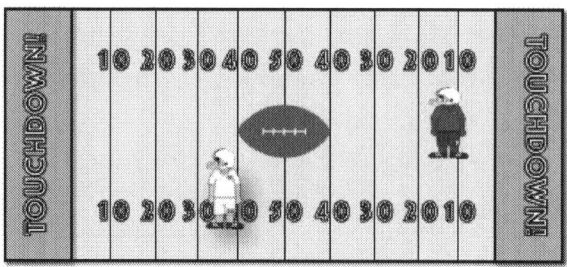

Other personal interests that have crept into my classroom have included (but definitely not limited to):

- Pirates – *"How's my sailing?" databases*
- Table top Gaming – *Design & code a dice game*
- Dungeons And Dragons – *Code your own adventure*

- Pirates (again!) – *Captain Vane's 'More Boats' Company*
- Marvel – *Our work is SUPER display boards*

Adding these personal touches will not only give you the personal motivation to be more creative, but will give students an insight into your life as a human outside of teaching. When you become more accessible, you become more than just a teacher that's telling them what to do.

## 19. Award tiny trophies

In a similar way to book stickers, having a drawer full of tiny trophies meant for party favours that I bought from a supermarket appears to work with almost every year group.

Team challenges are a useful tool for getting the energy higher up in a room and nothing has worked better than the exam question relay in recent years. Now, I cannot take credit for this idea as it actually came from my maths colleague Debbie:

In this game, an exam paper is printed and cut up into individual questions which are handed to a small team of students one by one (one paper per team). As the team answers the question together, they hand over their answer to the teacher for marking – if the answer is wrong, points are deducted, but no matter how many times they submit the question the marks are only awarded once giving the potential for minus points. The next question is only handed out once the previous question scores full marks.

As a fun way to get them to practice their exam technique, this works for all levels of students from primary SATS to A Level. Adding to this an element of deducting points if they hand in an incorrect answer slows them down and prioritizes accuracy over speed.

With a live (spreadsheet) scoreboard on the smartboard that is updated as we mark each team's answers, the winning team at the end of the session creates competition across the class.

My own touch to this is to award the team with the most points at the end one of my tiny trophies and a group photo on the wall until the next group challenge.

## 20. Stop and talk

This is something I have to remind myself about. It's all too easy to become overwhelmed by the workload and forget that the pile of books in front of us is actually the physical manifestation of the blood, sweat, and tears of our students.

I'm certainly not at my best prior to my second cup of caffeine of the day. Consequently, my students often get a "morning!" that is less perky than they often deserve. Because of this, I have a written reminder in my planner each day to have an off-topic conversation with one student every day (I know! Ofsted would have a fit!).

Conversations range from what games I play, to letting them know that I also struggle with resilience in the face of a "not perfect" grade, to explaining why my life on wheels is better than on legs. Talking to them off topic may not seem a productive use of my time, but creating a connection may just open up a communication channel that they need to talk about worries they have about their work.

# I Do Not Negotiate With Terrorists

After the fluffiness of the previous chapter, it's perhaps time to get down to some serious business. Even with the smallest of classes, teaching is not going to be all sunshine and rainbows. Some days classes won't behave, and some children will exhibit behaviour that you simply cannot tolerate. We cover these overt pushing of the boundaries later in Chapter 10, but what about that child that won't complete the task? How do we deal with the serial homework avoider?

The phrase "I don't get it" makes my blood boil but is often indicative of a survival mechanism. Students who have been in a system that tells them failure is a bad thing (sadly more true of our current system than ever now) will actively avoid personal failure by checking out of the system. But how do we encourage failure in a system where a test is a pass or fail?

This returns us back to the micro learning moments where we can influence a student's long term engagement with the outcome of a very short term task.

**Problem:** Max is not reading the question when asked to write an essay and often just hands in a few scrappy lines that were clearly written just before the lesson.

*All too familiar?*

**Micro moment**: 5 minute write. Given a big question, students are rewarded for quantity – every 60 seconds, students check their word count (easier in computers!). If they increased the word count by 50%, throw them a sweet.

Notice on here that Max stands a chance for a positive micro moment. He may have only written 10 words in the first 60 seconds, but if this only goes up to 25 by minute 2, then he is rewarded for working 50% harder. This differentiation of reward allows every student the chance for praise because it's personal.

Another less frantic way to banish the don't get it's is to harness peer feedback. It's not just about marking each other's work either – sometimes students provide some of the best formative feedback.

## 21. Create a class dojo

This free classroom digital reward system is great. Although it was initially launched for primary, it's equally useful in secondary school and mainly because it focuses on rewarding positive behaviour and gamifies your classroom by adding badges and collectables.

This isn't actually a section about this particular tool, but the use of gamification for behaviour. Short term rewards for positive behaviour create a kind of snowball effect and by adding tangible rewards like badges for progress is a catalyst.

This could be implemented in any number of ways from a spreadsheet, to beans in a jar – anything that allows them to see that their positive actions are noticed and will benefit them.

## 22. Use a flowchart for consistency

Of course, as a computer science teacher, flowcharts make me happier than they have any right to. However, a simple flowchart on the wall can help you to set clear boundaries for behaviour.

When a student swears in your class, rather than involving yourself in a long debate on whether that is appropriate ask them to consult the chart. "If you swear, what is the consequence?". Now the onus is on the student to tell you what the consequence is of their behaviour.

Pupil: *What the fuck?*

Teacher: *Charlotte, what does the chart say about using bad language in my classroom?*

Pupil: *If you swear, you have to...[consequence]*

Teacher: *So as you swore, what do you need to do?*

Pupil: *I have to ...[consequence]*

Teacher: *Thank you. Please go and [consequence].*

The result here is no shouting or losing tempers, but a direct consequence to actions that is difficult to dispute so creates minimal disruption to the lesson.

No debate, no bad feelings – just cause and effect.

## 23. Add SNOT to your classroom

3B4ME (The trendy version of "three before me") is a popular method employed in many classrooms where students are expected to try three things before asking the teacher for help, but often students come unstuck knowing where to access these 'three things'. My own preference is to use SNOT; if only because it sounds disgusting & for that reason alone kids love it. The added bonus here is that the acronym tells the students what to try.

**S**elf – the student pauses and talks their way through the problem. This is a technique that stems from programming called "Rubber Duck Debugging". If the programmer explains it to the literal rubber duck on their desk[4], they'll often realise what they did wrong before having to ask for help.

**N**eighbour – the student asks one of the people around them for advice (not the answer!)

**O**ther – the student consults another source, such as a text book or the internet.

**T**eacher – once all self-help avenues have been tried, the student approaches you with what they have tried and what the problem appears to be, rather than "I don't get it".

---

[4] This is genuinely a thing!

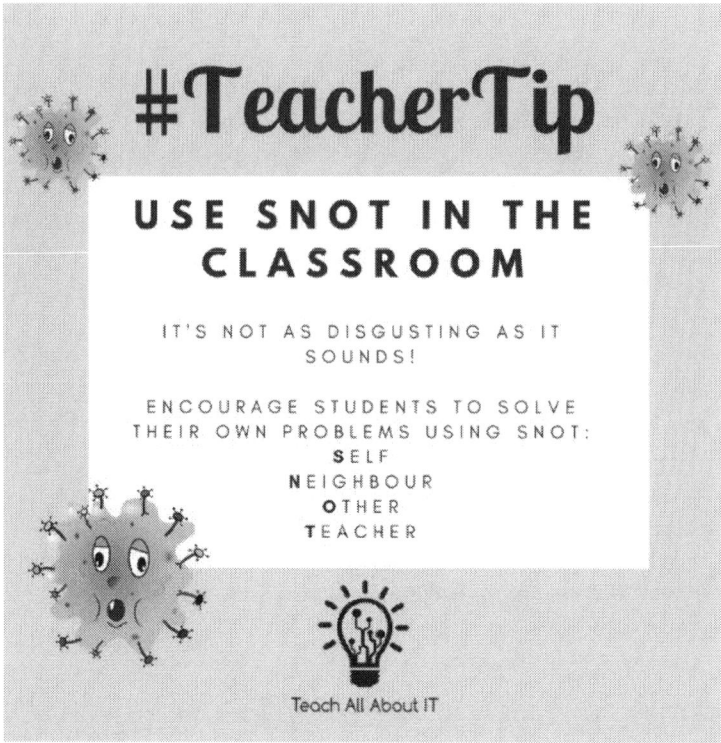

## 24. Ban hands up

Another reason students give for not making progress is that they had their hand up so couldn't get on whilst they waited for the teacher to notice. This is not a criticism of you as a teacher – an hour lesson gives you under 2 minutes to speak to each child in a class of 30.

One method that I employed was to stick "help" lights to each desk. These were a set of cheap battery powered push lights. When a student needed my help, they pushed their light and I had an instant visual of who needed help.

The bonus of this method is that they retain both hands for attempting another area of the task or a different question whilst they waited.

## 25. Make homework pegs

Whilst I still love my spreadsheet of handed in homework, one particular class had a subject where homework was more appropriate as a handwritten sheet each week. This class provided me with some of the most creative reasons that homework hadn't been completed and I found myself with a line of them at the start of each lesson.

Homework pegs were a simple idea that cured the line of excuses and gave me an instant visual of missing work:

Each child has a named wooden clothes peg on the board, attached by my trusty glue gun, or gluing a drawing pin to one side – as homework is put into the tray for marking, they attach the peg. Cue both named homework *and* a list of students I'd be spending lunchtime with!

## 26. Use behaviour bracelets

As a primary school behaviour technique, this is second to none. It also works surprisingly well for sixth formers...

This printable allows you to create a set of paper bracelets, much like you would see at a concert or festival. Each bracelet identifies a positive behaviour that they have exhibited.

This visual reward becomes an instant collectable in your classroom with students leaving school and sharing with parents. With a simple printable and a handy glue stick to stick the ends together, this becomes a sought after, but affordable tool in your armoury of praise.

For students who have some way to go, we can also use these as a target bracelet with a positive spin. "I'm going to put my hand up to join the conversation in tomorrow" – staying positive, gives them a target rather than the bracelet being a punishment.

## 27. Send notes home

In the same way as the behaviour bracelets create a link between you and parents, notes home create a similar but more direct link.

My notes home spreadsheet was born of my first meeting with a year 10 class who announced to me that I'd never teach them anything. Challenge accepted.

Writing a set number of emails home each day sounds like a management directive straight from the bowels of hell. And if you need to do this manually, it probably is. However, having a set of mail merged emails that you can add to a spreadsheet and have speed off at the touch of a button makes life much happier.[5]

The feedback from parents was incredible, and after a few weeks of emails shot out after each class, the behaviour began to improve and work started to be handed in.

Scan the QR code to download a template of the notes home spreadsheet and mail merge emails.

## 28. Gather student shout outs

In the social media world, a shout out is simply being mentioned by name in a positive way. We all love to be recognised for the good things that we do, but as teachers we don't always see every little thing that happens in our classroom. Student shout outs give us a double whammy of being able to praise students and encouraging them to be positive about other people.

This can be as simple as a shoebox style 'post box' and a block of sticky notes where students can post in a positive comment about someone in the room, or a board where the students can post their shout outs (I love the speech-bubble shaped post-it notes for this activity). Rather than making this a forced exercise, try combining it with the 'exit ticket' strategy below.

## 29. Plenary exit tickets

These were all the rage a few years ago and died a rather undignified death after they were used as a tick box exercise. However, in the hands of that student who flies under the radar, these can be invaluable.

Just like the Student Shoutouts above, a quick exit ticket handed in at the end of the lesson where students can choose what feedback to give can be incredibly powerful.

Give them a choice to tell you something positive, ask a question, or set a target for what they'd like to achieve next lesson. This will help you develop a pattern of which students need help or encouragement, and because it's

---

[5] *Before creating a sheet of contact details, check your school's data protection policy on holding contact details.*

direct to you it can also be a useful way to open up communication with students who are worried about their ability or showing signs of stress.

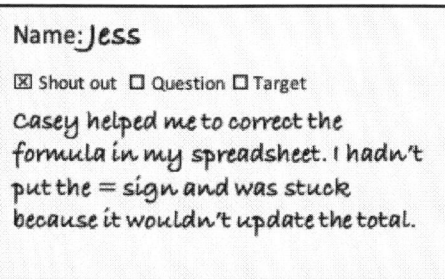

## 30. Technical noise

Noise in the classroom can sometimes be a catalyst for learning, and there is nothing better than the productive buzz of a class completely absorbed in an activity (not even cake). However, kids are not always the best at self-regulating their noise levels and this can make it intrusive and hamper their progress. In other cases, we may have a student in the class who has trouble with sensory processing and who finds high noise levels distressing.

Whatever the reason behind limiting the volume in the classroom, we can all agree that shouting doesn't work. We've all tried it.

Teacher: *Right! THAT'S ENOUGH! I want you all to work QUIETLY.*

Student: *Well, why are **you** shouting then?*

*Good point little person. Well played.*

Some teachers choose to have a noise meter on the board that they move around to identify the level of noise that they expect at that time. But, I personally find them cumbersome and ultimately forget to change them. My personal preference is to enlist technology to do the work for me.

One of my current favourite tools is the Too Noisy browser app is free and uses a microphone to detect the noise levels in a room. Teachers can set their thresholds which is great for switching from quiet work to class discussions. Scan the QR code to download the Too Noisy App.[6]

---

[6] *No payment was made for this recommendation, I really do like it!*

# You've Got The Music In You

Go on. Read that without humming…

Couldn't do it? That's possibly because music speaks to unconscious parts of our brains and sets a mood that continues long after the song has ended (especially if that song is an ear worm that gets stuck in your head for days!).

Music can be harnessed for long or short activities. How many times have you remembered a TV program or event you attended when you hear familiar music? Was that music even specifically related to event? Probably not unless it was a concert. It was likely there to enhance the mood.

You can use the psychology behind film music in your classroom by setting the tone of your class with entrance music. Are you covering a historical topic? Play some entrance music that relates to that time period. Want your students to work quietly? Play instrumental music that feels calming.

All that seems perfectly obvious, but there are other ways that you can implement music into your lessons that have a far deeper impact on learning.

## 31. Get cross curricular

If you're skipping past this chapter because you're thinking "well, I'm not a music teacher", stop right there. Yes you. Back here please. Take a seat.

Whether you teach Geography, Maths, MFL, or Science, music can be harnessed to make your lessons have an impact. In his research report for Centre for Education Economics, Gabriel Heller-Sahlgren suggested that students learn more from traditional 'chalk & talk' methods instead of fun. Since then, numerous reports have picked apart his evidence, showing that engaging lessons are far more effective for deeper, long term learning that can be applied instead of simply regurgitated.

Music is a wonderful way for teachers across the entire spectrum of the curriculum from primary to sixth form to set the mood for a lesson, a topic, or even a whole term. I'm not suggesting that you sing & dance at the front of your class (you could, but there's a strong possibility that you'd end up in a crumpled heap by the end of term shouting *"are you not entertained?"* – Entertainment is not the same as engagement, but there are aspects of one in the other.

There is an element of almost every subject in music, which means that you can harness music to teach a whole host of topics. With fewer students experiencing traditional music lessons, discovering the relevance of music through another subject can benefit both student and teacher.

Math

LangUages

HiStory

ReadIng

SCience

Rhythm and tempo in music can be directly attributed to maths work. At its most basic level, listening to a piece of music to work out how many beats per second (and consequently, per minute) are used in the song meshes both subjects. Now add in PE, and you can work out if a sing is best used for running, walking, or cooling down.

Consider the lyrics used in different songs – where did the language come from? Does it use metaphors, similes? Does it tell a story? Is it in fact, poetry?

Science is the one that people often look at and wonder how music could possibly be connected. However, if you haven't come across Festival of The Spoken Nerd, and Helen Arney's Sun Song scan the QR code because you're in for a treat!

## 32. Mix Music and Art

In fact not just art, but a technique for writing too. Give students free reign with content, but play a specific piece of music which they link to the work that they are creating.

This is a technique borrowed from art therapy where the music evokes a feeling which is then translated onto paper in a piece of artwork. In art, students use a variety of techniques to create a visual representation of the emotions portrayed in the music.

This could be translated into a number of different subjects, from a piece of creative writing based on the same method to developing a digital advert that uses the emotive music linking business studies and IT.

### 33. Introduce a student song of the week

With everyone having different tastes and backgrounds, this gives us the option to expand student's experience of music whilst potentially prompting cultural discussions. Rather than choosing their favourite song, ask students to pick a song that represents their family or something personal.

In any number of topics, the song of the week could be themed. My students enjoy seeking out the loosest references possible to technology looking for key words in the lyrics, but absolutely own the task.

Whilst this has the potential to spark an amazing array of conversations, you may want to check the songs first before you blast out the Peppa Pig theme tune, or much worse at the start of an observation!

### 34. Deploy the theme music!

I'm Batman. No, seriously. Or at least in my head, there's a theme tune playing as I enter the classroom to fight the crime of not handing in homework. As pleased as I was after my CAS Master Teacher[7] training, I will admit to being a tiny bit disappointed that I didn't get a cape.

Creating a theme tune for your classroom requires a bit of preparation, and is best done with new classes at the start of the year. This is a short piece of music that plays at the start of every lesson whilst they get settled. The idea here is that you've set the tone, they know where they are, and they better get settled in and ready by the time the theme music is done because the show is about to start!

With this said, it's important to choose the music wisely and not have your students dancing around the classroom, or cringing at the first few bars because it's become a dreadful earworm. The best example of this that I've seen was from a primary school teacher who used the tune of London Bridge Is Falling Down to prompt her students into cleaning up the classroom at the

---

[7] *Computing At School Master Teachers are subject leads who support other Computing teachers across the country. You can find more at www.computingatschool.org.uk*

end of the day. Not only did the song inspire positive action, the group bond that it created was nothing short of amazing:

*Tidy up now everyone*

*Everyone (eye contact), Everyone,*

*Tidy up now everyone*

*It's nearly home time!*

It became a welcome theme tune for her class, and the children remembered her fondly for it. Ten years later and the children that were in her class still sing it when tidying their room!

By making this a positive experience, this particular teacher avoided potential criticism of this technique from parents and students alike. Used inappropriately, this can shivers down the spine of any primary teacher – but when harnessed with enthusiasm and kindness (and a tune that won't haunt your dreams), this can turn you into a veritable Mary Poppins.

## 35. Use music as a timer

Many schools will be looking at pace within a lesson, especially in observations and there is simply nothing worse than a teacher (or student) constantly looking at the clock. Employing sound effects in your Smartboard™ presentations allow you to integrate pace and time management whilst looking like a pro.

When specific activities have a time frame, try adding a countdown timer to your presentations by creating a set of shapes with the minutes written on them, then placing them on top of each other (with 0 at the bottom), then adding an animation that hides the shapes every minute accompanied by a sound effect. This creates the effect of a timer, but embedded into your presentation. If you use this often, you can theme these sound effects to the time of year that you're using them.

## 36. Use sound effects

As a caveat to this, I will add *in moderation*. Much like using sound effects and music as a timer, embedding sound into presentations really can have an impact if used properly. Unfortunately, so many of us have been traumatized by overuse of the embedded PowerPoint animation sounds that we've been put off for life!

Sound effects for impact are less about drawing attention to a whizzy animation, and more about engagement. One teacher showed me their use of a clickable button in the corner of their presentation slides – when a student got a correct answer, the student was allowed to go up and press the button which generated a random sound. If the students are all working independently at the time, this doesn't impact on the pace, as only the one student is out of their chair. In fact, the pace is often increased because motivation improves.

This concept originally came from sales teams who would introduce a bell that was run every time a sale was made – this had the effect of highlighting praise for the person making the sale and sparking competitiveness in others in the room.

… Just like Pavlov's dogs, the sound of the bell prompts our brain to reproduce the feeling of success.

## 37. Weaponize the Christmas music!

Having been regaled with tales of the teacher who played "I want a hippopotamus for Christmas' on repeat for an hour in response to a lack of homework, I fully subscribe to the idea that Christmas music is not always as fun as it could be. Themed music can be used for good or evil, and there is no shortage of seasonal music throughout the year.

Nothing says *evil teacher* like "I'm Walking on Sunshine" right before a revision session. However, the less traumatic way of using this is to agree to play music for the final part of the lesson with a sliding scale of awfulness depending on the behaviour / productiveness of the lesson.

When employing this technique with my students we agreed a sliding scale. This is not to say that this is a definitive list, but an example of how they ranked what they wanted to hear (this was compiled as a quick survey):

**Amazing behaviour** – *All I want for Christmas* (with added singing)

**Good behaviour** – Fairy-tale of New York (safe version)

**Ok behaviour** – Slade's Merry Christmas

**Questionable behaviour** – The Snowman

**Terrible behaviour** – … *release the hippopotamus!*

## 38. Turn their music on them

You can almost guarantee that as soon as a song gets popular, a parody will be made. And if your subject happens to be part of the parody, hold onto that song and milk the life out of it!

Some subjects are luckier than others in this respect, and science tends to be heavily weighted towards an array of wonderful (and terrifically funny) songs that explain concepts in a light-hearted way. Of course, if you're that way inclined you could create your own parody or set this as a challenge to your students.

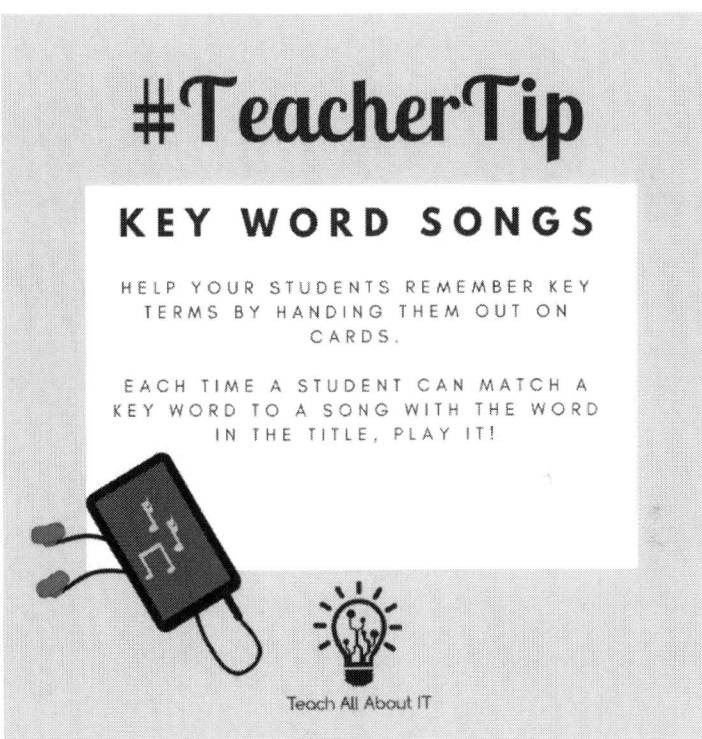

Adding key words to well-known songs is a great way to create an ear worm that will have the kids humming your revision notes for weeks!

For example, whilst learning about Trigonometry, one of my students was struggling with the key words as English was not her first language. She was however, very much enjoying the sound track of the musical Hamilton. By combing the two, we developed a rather unusual song for her to sing:

*Maths has trigonometry*

*For angles that we cannot see*

*SoHCaHToA will be helping me*

*Cos Sin Tan*

*Yes it can!*

For those not sure about the song, this was sung to the chorus tune of Alexander Hamilton. Scan the QR code to listen but be warned you'll be humming this forever!

As an example of turning kids onto learning about history, there is no better example.

## 39. Use familiar music

Just reading this, I can almost hear my year 11s cheering as the Countdown to Revision presentation plays the theme music from the long running TV show of the same name. Using familiar music can create an instant hook for students, but as with the previous tips with great music, comes great responsibility – the audio is the hook, not the content!

Much of what we do is selling the love and usefulness of our subject to our students. Learning how to critically analyse a poem is giving them the skills to look deeper into why that Facebook ad that seems just be a post is actually trying to sell them something. But what inspired them to look at the poem in the first place? What created the positive micro-moment that triggered the transfer into long term memory?

Potentially it was associating it with music that they also felt positively towards. Suddenly hearing the do do do do dooo of the revision presentation loading indicates that we've moved to an active part of the lesson and it will not just be learning, but with a bit of fun too.

## 40. Communicate differently

It would be remiss of me to have a chapter based on sound without adding an alternative that can be used for students who cannot access sound. When I lost a large part of my hearing in my early 30s it was terrifically difficult to adapt – a large part of adapting has been down to some amazing technology.

If you just had a flick through your SEN data and saw no kids with hearing loss, and those that do have hearing aids, pull up a metaphorical chair! Hearing aids make things louder – not clearer. And lots of us switch them off because they're overwhelming (shh.. don't tell my audiologist!)

One in three children will experience a form of hearing loss for 4 or more weeks during their school lives. And if the loss isn't permanent, it likely won't be on your SEN data. This is enormous and has a significant impact on learning.

So how do you implement sound aspects when there is a child with hearing loss in your class?

Almost any activity can be adapted for a child (or teacher) with a disability by being a bit creative. Let's be honest – being creative is what teachers do best. Let's adapt all the tips above for the kids who have hearing loss without detracting from those who can hear you:

**Tip #31 – Cross curricular**: *if you're using lyrics, consider learning the Sign Spoken English[8] for them. This will give another dimension to remembering the words which will also benefit all students because of the kinaesthetic aspect of signing to a song.*

**Tip #32 – Music & Art** : *tempo can be felt as well as heard. Give your student a speaker that they can feel. Just because someone is deaf, doesn't mean they can't get their groove on.*

**Tip #33 – Song of the week:** *Don't assume that your deaf students won't have a favourite song. They may want to introduce it as a video though – look out for the signed versions of songs on YouTube.*

---

[8] *Sign Spoken English uses the signs from British Sign Language, but uses the grammatical structure of spoken English.*

**Tip #34 – Deploy the theme music!** : *Add some actions to the theme. Jazz hands clearly end a song and double up nicely as the BSL[9] version of clapping!*

**Tip #35 – Use music as a timer:** *If you're using an audible timer, complement this with a visual timer on the board – if you don't want to add pressure by having a countdown clock, have a flashing symbol on the board to visually grab their attention.*

**Tip #36 – Use sound effects:** *This is a tricky one as the sound effect is a complementary tool in this tip. However, where I have students who are profoundly deaf, or who may miss on the subtleties of sound, I add some text to the presentation in the style of a closed caption to indicate what the sound was.*

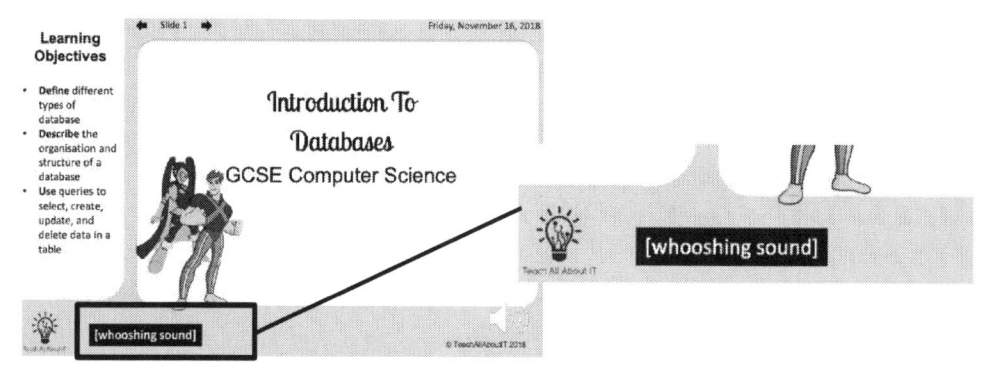

**Tip #37 – Weaponize the Christmas music!** : *This may actually be one of the perks of hearing loss. Can't stand the noise? Hit the off switch! Just like before, if you're rewarding the class with a Christmas song, play it as a signed video.*

*YouTubers like Jessica Kellgren-Fozzard have produced an array of signed songs that you can use in the classroom.*

*Scan the QR code for a festive example.*

**Tip #38 - Turn their music on them:** *This works with most students because the focus is on the lyrics rather than the audible music. The down side comes when you are reliant on the rhyme – but using rhythm works the*

---

[9] British Sign Language

*same. Consider instead learning the signs for the key terms in your topic. All students will benefit from the visual element of remembering the word as hand gestures trigger a response in our brains to create a connection.*

**Tip #39 – Use familiar music**: *This is a tough one - however, all is not lost. The purpose of this tip is to prompt recognition and this can be achieved in a number of ways: use the same colour scheme as the film, or program that the music comes from, design a similar logo, anything that visually links to the music and creates inclusivity.*

# Work For Idle Hands

Remember I said that you were funny? Well, believe it. But you're not just funny, you're interesting and you have important knowledge to impart. And yet somehow, they don't appear to be listening!

*But are they?*

Think back to the last seminar or lecture that you attended. Did you consistently make eye contact and nod along? Probably not. In fact, you were likely doodling on paper and making a spider web of notes that you had to decode later on.

In 2016, the Harvard Medical Journal wrote about the memory benefits to doodling for memory retention. They suggested that the act of doodling, a form of fiddling, reduced the stress on the brain that is caused from focused attention. This reduction then allows short term memory connections to be made for things that don't actively interest us.

The authors took this a step further, suggesting that doodling not only increases our ability to remember, but relieves daily psychological distress by mentally 'filling in' the missing gaps in short term memory and creating visual puzzle pieces which allow us to make sense of our lives.

So how can this be applied in the classroom?

Imagine for a moment that you are one of the young people sitting in your class in the last period of the day. You have woken earlier than your body is designed to do, been ushered into a building with many other people who you may not choose to befriend, and you are expected to sit attentively for the past 5 hours outperforming your previous academic standards. It's likely that you are worried about any number of family members or friendship, but you are currently faced with an hour of learning for the fifth, or perhaps sixth subject of the day.

Despite the posters on the wall informing you that you must arrive to all lessons prepared and ready to learn, you are most likely tired and fractious.

Generating empathy for your students in this way helps to adjust the techniques used at different times of the day and different points in the academic year. A lesson plan that went incredibly well period 2 on a Tuesday may very well be a huge flop period 5 on a Friday. This is not because you're a terrible teacher, but because we need to be just as adaptable as we expect our students to be.

## 41. Decorate Lesson Headings

In these afternoon lessons, one of the more interesting starters I have tried is a decorated heading. This is generally the centre of a mind map or the heading to some '*doodle notes*'. Give them just the heading and give them 5 minutes to present it beautifully with a tag line. This may not seem like a productive use of time, however in doing this students are thinking deeply about the words they are putting onto the page instead of scribbling volumes. You are creating a micro-moment of deeper learning.

## 42. Get them to draw your explanation

Doodle notes allow you as a teacher to make better use of what is now referred to as 'chalk & talk'. Lecturing from the front of the class has become something of a taboo in teaching and some observers even record the time spent at the front of the class. But what if you could make this an active experience? There is nothing wrong with talking to the class as a concept, the problem arises with extended talk where students have switched off. The solution to this is to chunk your explanations into 5 minute sections where they are engaged in recording the important snippets of information that you are imparting.

Notice that I didn't say '*writing*'; in fact, not all students will be comfortable with writing volumes, but they still have the capacity to record the main facts by using visual techniques.

## 43. Create doodle notes

Developing visual notes is a useful activity for students struggling with remembering terminology. By adding an image to their notes, they create a visual link in their memory that allows them to mentally navigate their revision.

# #TeacherTip

## LET THEM DOODLE!

ACTIVE LEARNING MEANS THAT THE STUDENT IS DOING SOMETHING WITH THEIR KNOWLEDGE.

CREATE STUDY NOTES BY USING A DOODLE PAGE - THE IMAGES WILL HELP WITH MEMORY!

Teach All About IT

This is not a single class activity, and you may find that you need to provide exemplars and feedback, so grab your fine-liners & colouring pencils!

**Doodle Notes 101:**

- Use plain paper & ink pens (have a class set for equal access)
- Create an illustrative title & tagline
- Identify key words in colour
- For each key term, add a doodle (could be a chart or just a sketch)
- Use talking time for main notes in black pen, then give them a few minutes DIRT to add more in colour.
- Keep notes safe! File them in classroom folders, stick them into books... whatever it is that you

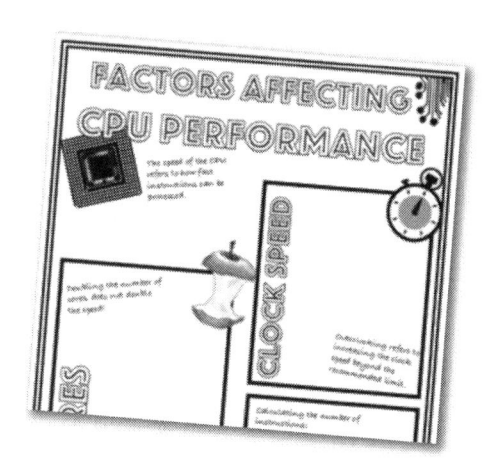

do, emphasize the importance of keeping them safe to increase their perceived value.

- When in doubt, use a template!

    o *To see how I use graphical notes for Computer Science, visit me at www.TeachAllAboutIT.school*

## 44. Colour code feedback for easy access *(stay with me here)*

The technique of using colour for different thought processes allows students to highlight context and additional areas, and you to assess their work flow. This is very different from the days of green pen – you are not asking them to respond to feedback but work at a higher level where they are self-correcting and enhancing before you give feedback.

Finally, when giving feedback don't write directly on their notes. Instead, add sticky note feedback, or paperclip a note to the paper. By treating their work as special and something you wish to preserve, you are generating passive praise which in turn encourages them to engage further next time you use the activity.

## 45. Doodle on a computer

Not everyone is an artist, but they can still create well presented notes. For students who struggle with written presentation, or as a differentiation and accessibility tool, try allowing students to make use of digital tools to doodle and create visual notes.

Help your students by creating a template which is scanned in as a PDF, then allow students to add to this by using free editing tools such as DocHub™ that allow them to type, free draw, colour, and ... doodle!

Scan the QR code to the left to try out DocHub[10].

## 46. 3D pull out notes

It's not just about colour and drawing but learning from the engagement that is generated by interactive content. Add an element of interactivity to student

---

[10] *As with other external links, these are not sponsored – simply tools that I find useful*

books by handing them concertina note templates to record the lesson content which can be folded and stuck into books.

One benefit of this is that the notes can be ordered to allow a concept and the detail to be revealed one after the other. This provides students with an instant revision tool.

### 47. Inspire them with decoration

Over the past few years, wall displays have taken on a life of their own and in part thanks to Pintrest™, classroom displays are a bit of a competition. Whilst it's amazing to have a Pintrest-worthy display in the classroom, they can be alarmingly expensive and cause us more stress than strictly necessary.

With that said… After spending a weekend with black sugar paper rolls, chalk pens, and many rolls of neon duck tape™ I welcomed my class back in on a Monday to be greeted with *'wow, I wish our other classrooms looked like this'*. Interestingly, that was the first year in many that I experienced only a handful of vandalism incidents in my room.

My balance came from creating a space in which to display few, but important notes that could be used when describing a concept – my walls became part of my lesson plan.

### 48. Develop a learning wall

Following on from decoration, another technique that combines decoration with the pull out notes in 46 is interactive displays.

These don't need to be all singing, all dancing, but could be as simple as pinning paper cups to the walls with extension activities that any students can pick up. Lolly sticks work brilliantly for this – write a generic task on a lolly stick, then as the student takes the task it is displayed on their desk. In this way, the teacher is aware of who has moved onto an extension.

Visual differentiation in action. The trick with learning walls is to be relevant to the class, and interactive.

### 49. Learn terms with revision rollers

Whilst remembering key terms and their definitions appears at the bottom of Bloom's Taxonomy, it does form the foundation of many of our subjects. Without the foundation knowledge, how do we apply, analyse, or create?

Revision rollers are a quick, but interactive way of creating revision dice that hold students' own notes. Concepts and definition are written on opposite sites of a 3D polygon which are then cut out and used as large revision dice.

Students can decorate these as much or as little as needed to create a visual and interactive set of notes, albeit ones that aren't particularly portable.

You can download a printable version of the rollers by scanning the QR code.

**50. Go for your pens!**

For some students, the phrase "a picture paints a thousand words" may not be as easy as they first think. A useful technique for making sure your students are listening is a quick draw.

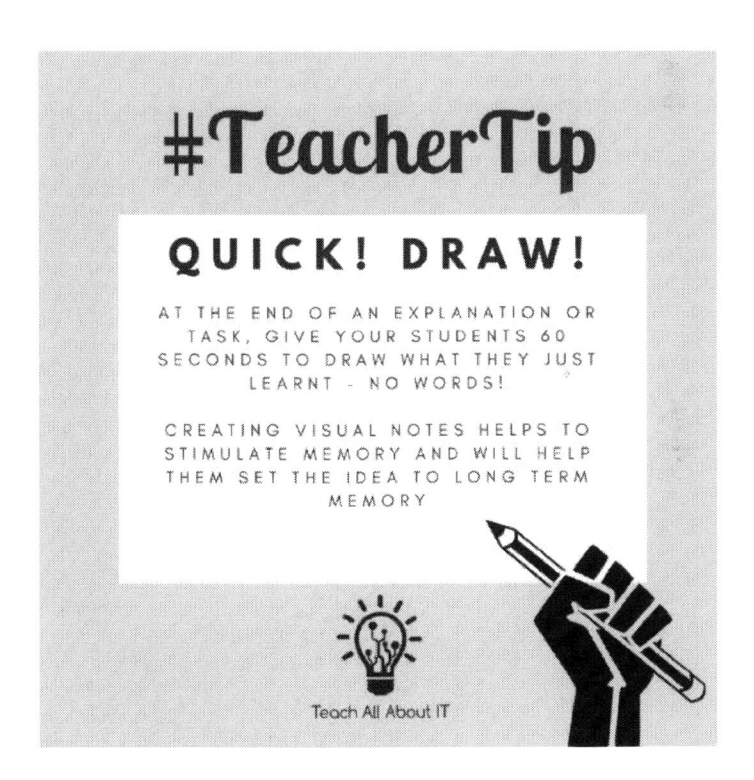

# #TeacherTip

## QUICK! DRAW!

AT THE END OF AN EXPLANATION OR TASK, GIVE YOUR STUDENTS 60 SECONDS TO DRAW WHAT THEY JUST LEARNT - NO WORDS!

CREATING VISUAL NOTES HELPS TO STIMULATE MEMORY AND WILL HELP THEM SET THE IDEA TO LONG TERM MEMORY

Teach All About IT

To add an interactive element to any teacher explanation, use mini whiteboards or scrap paper to give students under 60 seconds to draw the concept that you just described without the use of words.

This works on a number of levels – students no longer have to be concerned about spelling or handwriting, so engage more readily. This can be used to developed written notes where they can spend longer with a focus on these. Secondly, it creates a positive micro-moment combining an element of fun and visual memory techniques to help cement the concept.

*Of course, it also means that they'll be listening intently in case you ask them to draw again next time!*

## You Are Here

There are two ways that we can take our students on their education journey. The more traditional classroom sets you up as the train driver: you know where you are going and how to get there. Once they are on the train, aside from knowing the final destination they must trust that you know the way.

An alternative to this traditional method is the Sat Nav classroom. Ultimately, the destination is the same but they are shown the route in advance and given alternative routes with the possible change in journey time if they select the scenic route.

The Sat Nav classroom requires a great deal of pre-course planning, however much of this will be planning that you are already undertaking with your Scheme of Work. In this case, it requires some additions to the plan in terms of alternative activities where students can make a conscious choice as an individual or as a class to use one activity or another for a topic. This type of differentiation can be utterly terrifying for a teacher who is used to being in control or an NQT faced with a group of teenagers who know they are new. Interestingly, giving the class the illusion of control over the path creates greater engagement as this is now their activity.

In a similar way, sharing the planned path with a class is also a powerful tool for engagement. For several years now I have provided my students with a read only copy of my scheme of work for their course, explaining that this is our roadmap to get them to their exams and if they miss a class, or want to read ahead this is the tool that allows them to stay on our journey.

As teachers, this means that our schemes of work must be high quality documents. With lesson plans no longer in favour, our schemes of work have become detailed documents almost providing mini lesson plans with references to resources, activities, and homework.

### 51. Set practice style homework

Ah, homework. Nothing is better at dividing opinion than setting work outside of the classroom. In his book Visible Learning, John Hattie identified that in secondary school homework contributes to a positive upwards achievement rate in over 62% of cases and theorised that this could be improved further by setting specific types of task.

He discovered that the homework that had most impact in secondary was the tasks that focused on practice and closed end tasks. In fact, the more open ended the task was at higher levels the less impact it had whilst the opposite was true of younger years.

By setting clearer homework tasks at secondary and above, we are not spoon feeding, but creating an environment where the more reluctant students have a scaffold of what they much achieve, and the students at the other end of the spectrum have a defined end point.

## 52. Generate your worksheets

Teachers have enough to do without spending hours generating a unique set of worksheets for every student that allow them to practice all of the topics that have been set.

… but wouldn't it be nice if we could?

This is where the use of IT comes into its own. There are a multitude of tools out there that allow you to select specific questions, but a spreadsheet is often enough to create a 20 question random skills checker that will allow you to generate a custom sheet of your own short questions and answers.

You can download a template of the Skills checker generator by scanning the QR code. To use this for your own topics, go to the Questions tab and type in your own questions and answers. Once saved, go to the Printable tab, type in the number of students in your class and when you press the print button, a set of individual sheets with questions & answers will be printed for you!

## 53. Bulk set your homework

Letting our students know what is coming not only gives them a roadmap for learning but teaches them valuable time management skills. With this in mind, employing the tactics of social media gurus becomes possible. Knowing that homework tasks based on practice and specific knowledge will have the most impact on our students allows us to plan them well in advance.

> # #TeacherTip
>
> ## BULK SET YOUR HOME LEARNING
>
> SETTING HOMEWORK OVERWHELMING? LEARN FROM THE SOCIAL MEDIA EXPERTS & SCHEDULE HOMEWORK IN ADVANCE.
>
> YOU'LL SAVE YOURSELF TIME, AND KIDS & PARENTS CAN PLAN THEIR TIME
>
> Teach All About IT

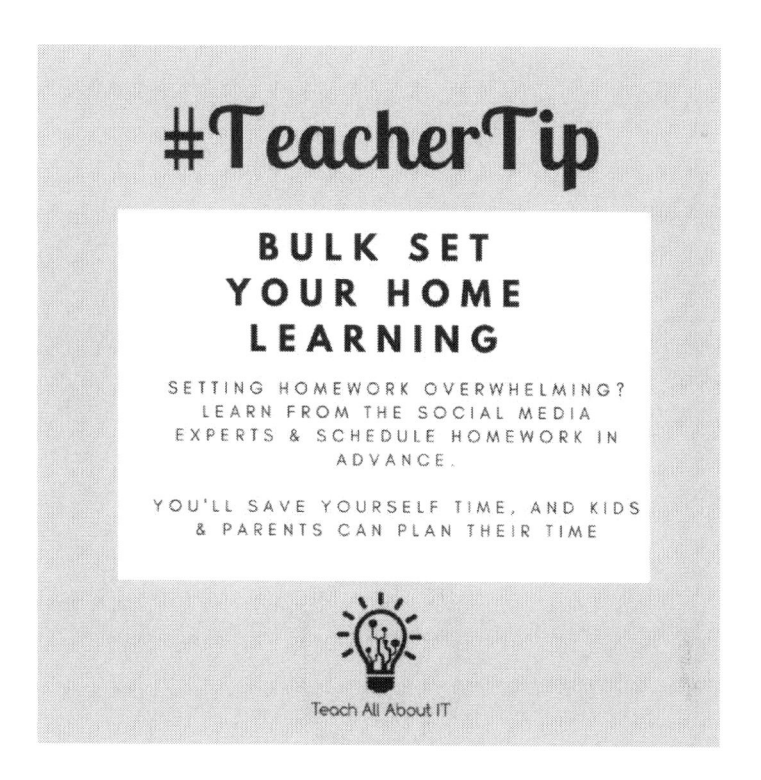

For many social media personalities, their following increases because they reliably provide content on a regular basis that meets a specific need. These people are not actually sat at their laptops hovering over the publish button at 10.25am every Wednesday. Instead, they use a time management skill known as bulk content creating where they create enough content for the following week, or even month and schedule its release using the technology available to them.

Whilst this may look overwhelming initially, actually spending one day planning homework for a half term, term, or even the whole year will actually save you time in the long run.

## 54. Only a fool breaks the 10-minute rule

This is no different to bulk creating homework tasks. Using the 10-minute rule we can estimate how long our tasks should take. The 10-minute rule suggests that a student should study at home for 10 minutes for every year they have attended school. Therefore, we could calculate using the following formula:

*Year 10 = 11 x 10*

*110 ÷ 9 (number of subjects)*

*= 12 minutes per night (rounded down)*

*12 x 5 = 60 minutes per week*

So here, I would be setting my year 10 class an hour of homework each week roughly divided into three areas: Practice, Investigate, Exam Questions. By making students aware of the 10 minute rule, you are arming them with context as to why they are required to work longer hours as they move up each year.

You are also setting clear boundaries of a maximum expected. Many students in the final years of GCSE and A Level (and into their working lives) have the impression that working hard equates to working longer. By setting a maximum time we are taking these students into consideration too and instilling a quality over quantity message.

Knowing how long I want my students to be working for alongside identifying the types of task that will have the maximum impact allows me to create a set of similar worksheets for each week of the year which reflect my scheme of work. Although this may appear to be deathly boring, students do in fact thrive on the regularity that they see with their social media icons. My homework task 'drops' every week at the same time and day because I use technology to schedule it in advance (I'd last under two weeks if I did it all manually!). Using tools like Moodle, Google Classroom, Edmodo, or Show My Homework means that you can spend a day creating your worksheets and scheduling them a half term, or even a term ahead and appear to be the most organised teacher going.

Each week, their homework is 'checked in' to ensure that it is complete, but assessment remains on the schedule (see next chapter). This purposeful practice is one of our vital tools in the toolkit to covering the vast quantities of information required in the new style exams.

We're not working harder – we're working smarter.

## 55. IT room tech

If you happen to be in an IT room that uses software to monitor screens, you'll be familiar with the collective groan every time that you take over their screens. In fact, after the initial amazement from new students who occasionally think that you're either magic or a hacker, most students dislike the system intensely. But what if you could use it as your secret weapon to prod students into making more progress?

Most of these monitoring suites have the ability to sending messages direct to individual screens. During a quiet lesson, or an assessment, this could give you the opportunity to monitor the screens of a whole class and feedback in real time.

During a particularly tough IT assessment, I happened to notice one of my students becoming increasingly frustrated. They could see others around them had finished and they weren't nearing the end (in fact, they had plenty of time, but student's perceptions are different to ours). I sent the following pop up message to their screen:

> Don't panic. Just do your best 😊

I could see him physically relax, when he turned around, we smiled and he finished the test, with a great result.

Micro-moments don't have to be face to face. In fact, we live in a digital world so making use of the technology at our disposal to create human relationships is just an evolution of teaching.

You could use this in several other ways – in purposeful practice, suggest an extension, provide some formative feedback on a piece of work, create a silent revision disco…

## 56. Feedback sheets vs. progress sheets

The feedback debate in education may in fact roll on forever. There are volumes written about the most effective way to give feedback to students in order for them to improve work, become independent learners, and a whole host of other outcomes.

Because we give feedback for a number of reasons, if we try to fit our feedback into a set format every time, we are trying to push an educational square peg into a round hole.

After all that, you'd probably be surprised to hear that I'm actually quite a big fan for formalised feedback sheets. However, I like to use them as formative rather than summative. If feedback is summative, a grade or mark is sufficient. In contrast, where feedback requires an action I want the creative freedom to actually help.

I use online feedback more and more, and generally because I find that adding hyperlinks and videos allows my students to interact with their feedback in a way that they are used to through social media. That's not to say that I send their feedback via Twitter, but I take my styling cues from web design and marketing.

When designing web pages, adding in content making use of the Golden Ratio ensures that the page is aesthetically pleasing – just like the puppies and kittens in chapter 1, being given something that is nice to look at maintains our attention for longer.

The Golden Ratio is a mathematical principal that can be seen everywhere from nature, to science, in the Fibonacci sequence, and is used in design to create the optimum ratio of main content to side content.

In my feedback sheets, the main content is actually a screen capture or scan of their work. The feedback is generally a two stars and a wish style which is entered either into a spreadsheet, or typed into the document. This is then used as the basis of a DIRT session (see 5,4,3,2,1…. Blast Off!).

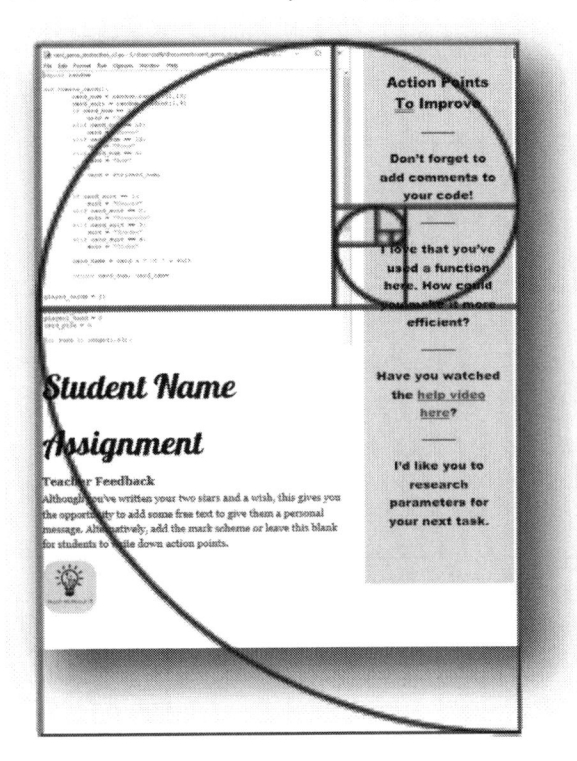

Once the template document was set up, I found marking in this way much easier as I was no longer scribbling on their work, but instead on a copy that they could take note of.

For students who are struggling with presentation, this also models a clear example – you can even share the secret of the Golden Ratio with them!

## 57. Keep them on their toes

Whilst your scheme of work should be structured, you don't have to be. In fact one of the few student complaints that bothered me over the years was that I don't stand at the front of the class and teach in the structure of the textbook.

Anyone who has taken a breath in my classroom will know that perfunctory chalk and talk is not my style. It would make life very dull indeed and how do you inspire a group of teenagers to love the inner workings of a laser printer without a bit of creativity?

My scheme of work will be very clear about the topic and the learning outcomes, but arriving in my classroom my students will never be sure if they'll be creating a megalithic poster of program code, or dancing an algorithm.

If students are aware of the required outcomes and can identify the progress that they have made on a personal level, there is absolutely nothing wrong with creating an entirely entertaining lesson.

One of my particular favourites has been 'revision twister' which included an actual Twister mat and a PowerPoint simulation which included an entire exam paper of questions.

You can download a copy of the presentation by scanning the QR code. Change the questions to fit your own topic, add a Twister™ mat and hey presto! Instant engaging revision.

## 58. Reverse engineering an exam

Exam technique is sometimes just as important as knowledge. Looking at an exam paper from the perspective of the examiner may feel a little bit like cheating, but just like previous methods, this technique allows students to focus on an end point for the current part of their journey.

For students who are feeling less confident with the material, this can be a particularly effective tool as it removed the fear of the unknown from the task.

Especially where essays are concerned, fear of the blank page can produce an effect much like a rabbit in headlights. Consequently, our students stop and make little progress. Instead, when dealing with longer answer questions, a mark scheme can be used as a writing frame. The physical act of writing out the long answer then creates a positive revision experience which they can use as the scaffolding of the mark scheme is removed.

## 59. Model a less travelled path

Think about how you ended up in your current role. More likely than not, you couldn't have predicted where you currently are ten years ago. So imagine how difficult it is to have a clear goal for a time almost your entire lifetime in the future, and a plan to get there.

When we give careers advice, we're likely asking our kids to prepare for a job that doesn't even exist yet in a world that will look very different to how it is now. If we prepare them instead for the courage and ability to change direction, we give them the self-confidence to become the entrepreneurs and self-starters that so many assemblies talk about.

Giving them those skills can sometimes be as simple as modelling that unusual path. We sometimes become so wrapped up in presenting a professional and totally in control image, that it's a real shock when we admit we've failed.

One of the most powerful conversations I've had in recent months was with a friend who has recently returned to university. I'm in absolute awe of her bravery to jump in feet first, but she believed that everyone around her had it absolutely sorted. So when I said that actually I'd dropped out of my A Levels because of my mental health it was a real shock.

In fact, I went back to university in my mid-twenties with two (very) small babies. But I too easily forget that actually sharing that with a student who sees a repeated year as a failure could well be the reassurance that they actually need.

If you don't want to share your own story, scanning the QR code will take you to a set of careers interview blogs that I created showing the wide and varied paths to careers that people never dreamed would become reality.

## 60. Show them the next level

This seems rather counter-intuitive at the start of a course, but actually many students will see the step up as progress measurement. You telling them that it's good progress is all very well, but do they really believe you?

Consider how many younger siblings measure their physical growth against their 'big' brother or sister. By setting a target point for the start of the next level, students can reflect back and ask themselves 'how much closer am I to this?'.

At the start of year 12, after just 3 weeks in class, I set my new students a group challenge. As a way to introduce this challenge I showed them a piece of work that year 13 were currently working on and set them an initial challenge of working together to research and teach each other just one thing from the example.

After the first assignment, each student was able to measure how much progress they'd made towards the next step – not because I'd told them, but because they could see what was coming next.

# 5,4,3,2,1... Blast Off!

Habits aren't formed overnight, but are difficult to break once they are properly formed. One of the bad habits that many teachers fall into in the first few years is to assume that every piece of work needs to be marked in detail and attempt to provide written feedback in a rainbow array of colours for every class each week.

In doing this, we are actually encouraging our students to become dependent on us to make progress. One of the most useful positive habits our students can develop is to self-assess and redraft their work, but this is often a hard won battle where students (and parents) have often come to expect the teacher to provide the exact path to success.

One of the most difficult transitions I made was reducing the frequency of marking for my classes and convincing them that less was in fact more. Over the course of a year, I reduced my marking frequency from once a week to twice each half term. Of course, I wasn't actually providing less feedback at all. Instead, the quick two stars and a wish hurriedly written in books each week was transformed into a piece of detailed formative feedback that could be used to identify improvements in future pieces of work.

This applies just as much to the marking of homework. With the knowledge from our last chapter that homework tasks are best suited to practice tasks, completion can be quickly checked by providing answers as part of a DIRT task within lesson time. This doesn't need to be detailed, but it should be regular – where answers are straight forward, providing a mark scheme allows students to practice self-assessing their answers whilst you are able to record whether a task has been completed.

### 61. Plan your assessments

One of the easiest ways that teachers can form the habit of less, but still regular feedback is to plan early. Assuming that you will be marking twice each half term for a class, the Scheme of Work can be used as a planning tool to identify twelve spaced out tasks that will be assessed. As a rule of thumb, these should be a variety of assessments that reflect the scope of the course.

## #TeacherTip

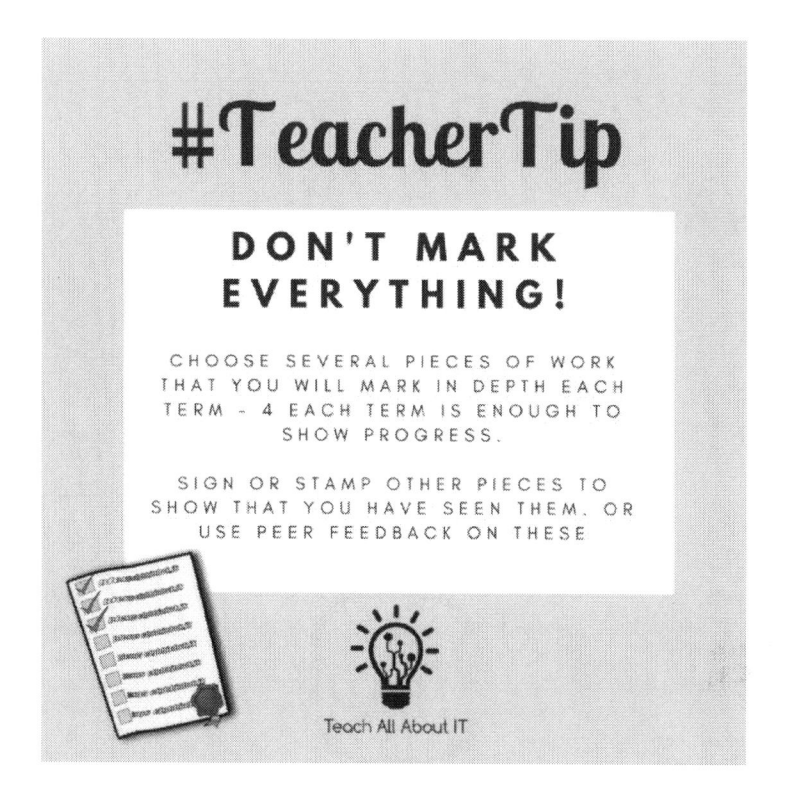

### DON'T MARK EVERYTHING!

CHOOSE SEVERAL PIECES OF WORK THAT YOU WILL MARK IN DEPTH EACH TERM - 4 EACH TERM IS ENOUGH TO SHOW PROGRESS.

SIGN OR STAMP OTHER PIECES TO SHOW THAT YOU HAVE SEEN THEM, OR USE PEER FEEDBACK ON THESE

Teach All About IT

Over the course of the year, you may choose to assess:
- 3 written tests
- 3 practical tasks (presentations / groups tasks etc.)
- 4 homework tasks
- 2 long answer questions

It's useful to give students fair warning that a task will be assessed. This not only encourages them to put additional effort into a task, but also helps them to form positive habits of preparation and revision without the high stakes of formal exams.

By planning your assessments for the year ahead (yep, the whole year!) and sharing these with your students you are providing clear information of what is expected of them. The first year that I completed this task, I was overwhelmed by developing a full year's worth of tasks and was convinced that my students would balk at being given a year of homework up front. I was stunned at the polar opposite reaction, with students openly telling me that they felt more confident with the tasks as they knew what was coming and that there were no nasty surprises around the corner.

## 62. Use a rubric

Infrequent marking also puts you in the excellent position of being able to design a marking rubric for each task which allows you to easily provide formative feedback and objective marks for a task. A simple rubric for a homework task from the previous chapter may look like:

|  | 0 marks | 2 marks | 4 marks | 6 marks |
|---|---|---|---|---|
| Practice Questions | Not completed | Most attempted / not full sentences | All attempted with mostly full sentences. | All completed with full sentences. |
| Research Task | Not completed / not own work | Questions answered & sources cited | Questions answered in detail & sources cited | Questions answered in detail with sources and quotes |
| Exam Questions | Not completed | Some attempted | Most attempted using P-E-E | All attempted using P-E-E |

Notice that in the rubric, the marks awarded are for the skills shown rather than the number of questions actually correct. Marking in this was for some (not all) assessments rewards both effort and ability and provides a positive experience for students who may well be achieving their personal best but are demotivated by lower grades.

I have celebrated the 4s & Cs with more enthusiasm than any number of 9s and As because of the blood, sweat, and tears it took to achieve them. Those students deserve to be rewarded for their positive study habits just as much as our academically gifted students.

Whilst many online tools allow you to set up marking rubrics, I will always favour the use of a spreadsheet as this allows you to set your task comments as a drop down list with each assigned a specific number of marks. If you happen to be a bit of a spreadsheet wizard, these can be used to create printable feedback sheets.

## 63. Use a mail merge

The feedback sheet in the previous chapter was often used in conjunction with a set of comments in a bank. Each time a student prompted me to come up with a new comment, this was added to the bank so it could be used again with another student.

Comment banks get a bad rep from teachers and parents for being impersonal and not particularly effective. When the comments are restrictive and applied across a whole school, then this is a valid point and they become words for the sake of words. However, you can harness the power of the comment bank with some nifty mail merge tricks that will ban the 'copy & paste' approach to writing reports whilst still giving you the safety net of a scaffolded sentence.

**Step 1:** Write down a list of potential generic comments that you want to include in your feedback or report. Where you intend to write the child's name use X.

**Step 2:** Create a spreadsheet with your kids' names along the left column and headings for each comment column.

**Step 3:** Use the 'Data → Data Validation' menu to create a drop down menu for each of the cells in the columns from the list of comments you created.

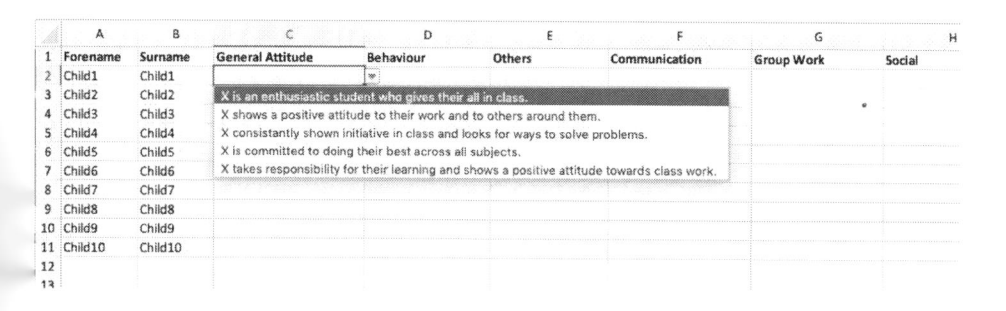

|   | A | B | C | D | E | F | G | H |
|---|---|---|---|---|---|---|---|---|
| 1 | Forename | Surname | General Attitude | Behaviour | Others | Communication | Group Work | Social |
| 2 | Child1 | Child1 |  |  |  |  |  |  |
| 3 | Child2 | Child2 | X is an enthusiastic student who gives their all in class. |  |  |  |  |  |
| 4 | Child3 | Child3 | X shows a positive attitude to their work and to others around them. |  |  |  |  |  |
| 5 | Child4 | Child4 | X consistently shown initiative in class and looks for ways to solve problems. |  |  |  |  |  |
| 6 | Child5 | Child5 | X is committed to doing their best across all subjects. |  |  |  |  |  |
| 7 | Child6 | Child6 | X takes responsibility for their learning and shows a positive attitude towards class work. |  |  |  |  |  |
| 8 | Child7 | Child7 |  |  |  |  |  |  |
| 9 | Child8 | Child8 |  |  |  |  |  |  |
| 10 | Child9 | Child9 |  |  |  |  |  |  |
| 11 | Child10 | Child10 |  |  |  |  |  |  |

**Step 4:** Select the most appropriate comment for each child for each of the headings. Once added, these comments can be adjusted and personalised until the cows come home, or you can wait and adjust them in Word.

**Step 5:** Create a mail merge into a Word document that brings in all of your comments from the spreadsheet into a word-processed document. To personalise them, press Ctrl + F (or cmd + F on a Mac) and replace all instances of X with the child's name.

If your reports have to be uploaded into a school-wide system, you can copy & paste. Otherwise, you can print them directly from the merged document.

## 64. Keep things digital

Although this may not be possible for every subject, for many this is a solution which means that you don't have to carry piles of books with you, the dog can never eat the work, and that third cup of coffee won't be going over your marking!

One of the best investments I made as a teacher and tutor was my laptop. The main feature that I looked for in the laptop was the ability to flip it over and use it as a massive tablet with a stylus. When combined with scanned copies of students work, I can add annotations and upload them to shared spaces.

## 65. Record your verbal feedback

This will feel very odd the first few times that you do it, but video and audio feedback allow you to provide far more detail in a short space of time than written feedback.

In instances where you need to provide the next step for improvements or extension, especially in coursework, adding an audioclip allows the student to pause you, make adjustments, and then return to your commentary just as if you were sitting with them.

If you're marking a PDF in Adobe Reader, click > Rich Media > Select Object to add an audio comment.

Alternatively, office applications often allow you to insert voice annotations into digital documents which can be embedded and listened to again later..

## 66. Video your top three class mistakes

I can see you cringing already. Think back to chapter 2 when we talked about why students announce "I don't get it" – avoiding video in a lesson is the teacher equivalent: If it's on video, you can't ignore the mistakes.

Videoing your lesson needs to be approached in line with your school or college's policy on recording students. If they use something like IRIS, grab it with both hands (carefully though, it's expensive). Alternatively, use a departmental device to create a recording.

Why not your phone? This just opens you up for a whole host of safeguarding issues and it's just safer from your perspective to keep your work and personal devices separate. Of course, if you're a tutor all you need is parental permission – and parents often encourage this so students can use the recording as revision.

Once you've tackled your fear of video, teach as you normally would. This isn't about formal observations, you want to reflect on what you genuinely do. You are going to be your biggest critic, so make a list as you watch back of all the good and all the bad.

Finally, pick the top three from both lists. These will be your top three targets to work on and also top three things to add as 'rinse and repeat'. Don't feel disheartened by having a list of things that went wrong; teaching is a craft, there is no teaching nirvana and it's a constantly changing environment. What you're doing is being open to change and embracing the power of Yet.

*Tom wasn't really paying attention... yet. But if I used a music based timer, he might feel more motivated.*

## 67. Record your mark scheme explanation

I am not a fan of marking everything, but I am a fan of effective feedback. When I set a test, I mark question by question taking a photo or scan of a student answer for each. Each student is selected for one answer to be included, but not identified personally.

The paper-based marking of their tests uses examiner notes and nothing else:

✓ *mark awarded*

✗ *incorrect*

P *point noted (useful in essays where a tick does not mean a mark)*

NE *not enough*

TV *too vague (similar to not enough, but where they're waffling)*

NAQ *did not answer question*

Even this set of marking points will give them a certain level of feedback that will reduce your time spent marking, but often we also want to include formative feedback, and this is where the photos come in.

Programs like PowerPoint have the option of adding voice recordings, or even screen recordings which can then be exported as videos. By adding your photo of a question and then recording you marking it on screen picking out positive points and areas for improvement, you can create a whole class feedback video for a test in under an hour for a GCSE paper.

Students have been really positive about these as they own the work, and can watch them back as revision for the next test, especially if the feedback is focused on exam technique.

## 68. Don't fear self-assessment

Self-assessment is a powerful addition to the workload toolkit. But this isn't just about reducing the time you spend sleeping on the exercise books. Think back to tip 61 where you are planning your assessment points – these are the assessments that you will mark and give feedback on, but that doesn't mean that students shouldn't get feedback on other work. It's just not formally from you.

90% of the homework that I set includes either a mark scheme or will be given a mark scheme on the due date. Doesn't this encourage them to just copy out the mark scheme? Yes and no.

Consider this: For the student who is struggling with the subject, is it better to set a question and make them show that they don't know, or allow them to reverse engineer the mark scheme into a valid answer.

Providing the end point and asking them to investigate how to get to the final answer creates a safety net and makes the task more positive because they aren't entirely in the dark.

This is much easier in open ended questions and essays as the points can be provided allowing them to structure them into a long answer. In subjects like maths, this could be reworded to ask them:

*Explain why 32 is the square root of 1000*

You're giving them the *what*, but not the *why*.

## 69. Create QR code stickers

Previously, I talked about the benefits of adding reward stickers to the front of books. Give your stickers an extra edge by printing them with a QR code of a useful resource to revise further, or mix this with a link to an extension task.

I've used QR codes extensively in this book to link you to helpful resources. If you'd prefer to link to a worksheet, create a cloud account that allows you to create shareable links to your resources. They are terrifically easy to create – simply type in 'create QR code' into any search engine and you'll be presented with a host of websites where you type in either text or a web address and hey presto, you just download the image.

QR codes allow students (and teachers) to use their phones to access more information. The ban of phones in schools baffles me in the extreme – we have a generation of students who have access to computers in their pockets and as an educational society, we herald them to be the root of all evil. They're not if we use them appropriately.

Adding QR codes to your wall displays, or even to handouts at a parents evening will reduce the need for printing and make your printables interactive.

## 70. Create a highlighter colour code

A caveat to this task – with one in three males in the UK having some form of colour deficiency in their sight, be careful not to use this as your sole method of feedback. Many students will have no idea that this is an issue for them and will miss your identification. Using a free app on your phone to check that your colours differ enough is advisable.

If much of your students work is hand written in an exercise book, then this tip is absolutely for you. Before commencing, it's useful to create a colour code key which is printed and stuck into their books which allows them to cross reference what the highlighting actually means.

Once done, all you need to do to include the repeated feedback in a student's book is to grab your highlighter!

Found an error in SPaG[11]? *Highlight blue.*

---

[1] SPaG – Spelling and Grammar

Incorrect answer? *Highlight orange*

Section for the student to reword or rewrite? *Highlight yellow.*

These are just examples and your codes can mean anything that is relevant to your subject, but it's a quick way to provide formative feedback that students will find clear and simple.

# Frankly My DEAR...

DEAR, or Drop Everything And Read is a bit of a marmite subject in most schools. On one hand, the idea of stopping and just reading for just 20 minutes each day sounds blissful, and on the other, have you *tried* to read a book in a room full of teenagers where 60% of them are trying to do anything but read?

In the three full academic years that I participated in a weekly DEAR tutorial & termly full hour lessons I probably read two chapters. My DEAR time was generally spent shushing students, confiscating phones, and reminding them that we weren't allowed to sit on the floor.

And yet, I still fully see the benefit in embedding this activity in every classroom. The issue wasn't in the idea, but the **execution**.

If you're going to implement a clear reading time in the classroom, then great! But...

### 71. Make reading regular

Weekly for under 30 minutes, and only when revision / homework isn't needed isn't going to cut it. A local school has embedded DEAR into their daily timetable with all students returning to their form rooms for 20 minutes each day. Because it is part of their daily routine, the students treat this time as a standard part of the school day and subsequent lessons are generally calmer and more productive.

This approach made it abundantly clear to students that time to read quietly was a top priority, so much so that it was in the timetable. Even the introductory day for new students included a 20 minute DEAR session where students could read anything they chose.

### 72. Make reading accessible

Not every student has an age appropriate reading level. Let them read comics, let them read graphic novels, encourage them to bring in enormous tomes with old pictures in. And where the student can't access the written word, provide them with headphones and an audiobook.

.. heck, play that audiobook to the whole class!

Audiobooks are not cheating. They provide a number of benefits that can be combined with the traditional ink on paper approach. Voracious readers gather a great deal of their vocabulary from the books that they read, but the English language has a nasty habit of including words that phonetically make no sense whatsoever.

To prove this, I asked the Twitter hivemind to give me real life examples to add to my own of 'Lieutenant' that took me years to match to hearing '*lef*tenant'.

> **J** @JThomEdu · Nov 11
> Replying to @TeachAllAboutIT
> "Hermione" for me! I said "Hermy-one" for the whole first book until I had an epiphanic conversation with my teacher and was corrected.

> **Mr C. Smith** @DebugEdu · Nov 11
> Replying to @TeachAllAboutIT
> Oddly enough it was always the names of characters. For example I have been a massive fan of discworld for many years and often don't connect "Detritus" with how it should be said, often saying it in my head as "Deitrus"

> **Thirsty: Cruel & unusual as standard.** @Thirsty_BTP · Nov 11
> Replying to @TeachAllAboutIT
> The big one was "grimace" a word that is almost never spoken.
>
> But also "bourgeoisie" which I did realise was a different word from "bourgeois" nobody corrected me for a decade as the two were used interchangeably.

Audiobooks bridge this gap, allowing us access to correct pronunciation (narrators spend hours identifying the correct pronunciation of words), and also allow provide an accessible access to books beyond the current reading capability of an individual. Much like a parent reading to a child, we never really grow out of enjoying being read to – it's why drama podcasts are so popular!

## 73. Read for both pleasure and purpose

There is a theory that children who see their parents read for pleasure will read more themselves. This is largely the case, however my own children are an interesting example of why this may not always be the case.

We are both avid readers of a wide variety of books, with family holidays dedicated to time to indulge in getting lost in any number of novels. Our eldest daughter has followed our example and has taken the concept of bookworm to whole new levels. In contrast, our youngest would rather remove her own toenails with a rusty spoon than read for pleasure. Regular DEAR time has benefitted both in very unique ways: providing one with the time to melt into a new book, and the other enforced structured time to accept that graphic novels aren't *that* bad.

After reading for pleasure has been established, reading for purpose is another vital skill. If you are struggling to identify where in your lessons you are embedding literacy, you need only look at the way in which the information is presented to your students.

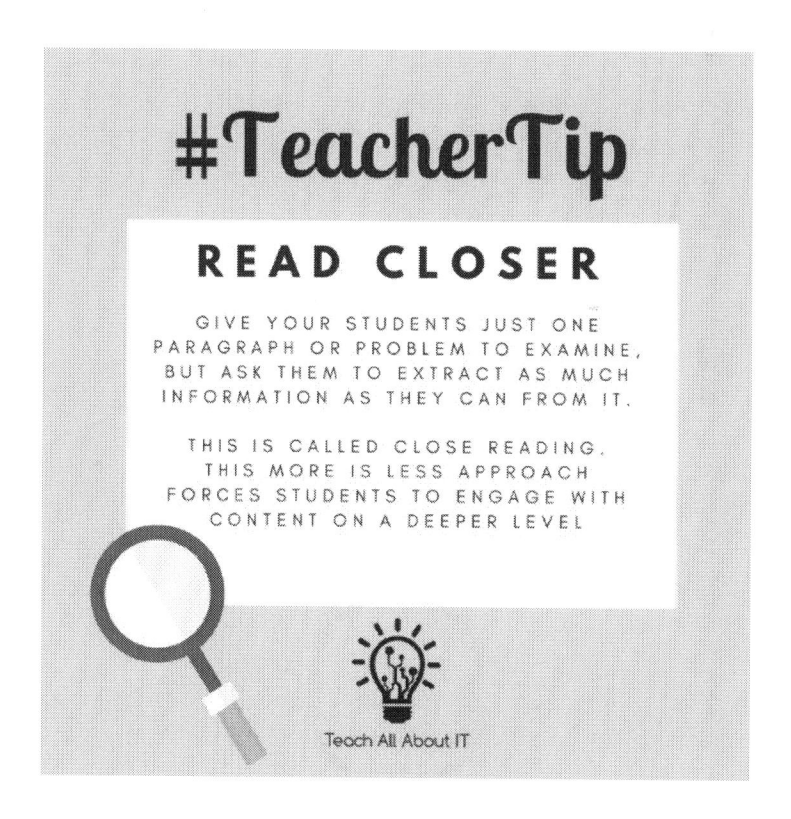

### #TeacherTip

**READ CLOSER**

GIVE YOUR STUDENTS JUST ONE PARAGRAPH OR PROBLEM TO EXAMINE, BUT ASK THEM TO EXTRACT AS MUCH INFORMATION AS THEY CAN FROM IT.

THIS IS CALLED CLOSE READING. THIS MORE IS LESS APPROACH FORCES STUDENTS TO ENGAGE WITH CONTENT ON A DEEPER LEVEL

Teach All About IT

A powerful starter task that can be used across the whole curriculum is known as Close Reading. Students are given a very small piece of information in pairs or small groups and asked to examine it in fine detail and extract as much information as possible. For a literacy link, this may be a single paragraph or quote where the inferred meaning is dissected.

Consider giving this quote to students as the starter to a PE lesson where students are discussing nature vs. nurture:

*"Do not let what you cannot do interfere with what you can do."* – John Wooden

Some students may concentrate on the sporting meaning of the quote, whilst others might be able to apply this to situations outside of the immediate context. Others may consider what makes this a particularly memorable quote from a literary perspective, or discuss the psychology of the words used for motivational quotes. It's surprising how much students are able to dig into a single sentence.

As a concept, close reading can be applied to any number of subjects. This may be providing a formula for mathematics, a set of statistics in geography, or a colloquial phrase in modern foreign languages.

Both reading for purpose and for pleasure benefit each other, and by creating both as an ongoing positive habit for our students we are benefitting their progress in our own and other subjects.

## 74. Widen your own reading

This is easier said than done. I am absolutely guilty of not reading for pleasure for months at a time during term time, and have been caught more than once poolside on holiday with an educational theory book in hand (generally by other teachers who spark up a conversation and laugh at never being 'off the clock').

However, getting stuck in a literary rut and being constantly on the clock isn' good for us. Just like making reading accessible for our students, considering how we get to access to our literacy fix sometimes requires some creative thinking.

If you're an early riser, why not stall getting up for 30 minutes and read in bed before other people in the house wake up? This allows you to read in peace while you are rested and will also have the added benefit of starting your day more relaxed and with something accomplished before you even put your bunny slippers on!

## 75. E-Readers are not the enemy

To borrow phrasing from Dr Seuss,

> *I do like reading, Sam-I-am!*
>
> *On a train! in a tree!*
>
> *In a car! Just let me read!*
>
> *I would, and could in a box!*
>
> *I would and could read with a fox.*
>
> *I would read e-books with a mouse.*
>
> *I would read print books in a house.*
>
> *I listen to books here and there.*
>
> *I enjoy them anywhere.*
>
> *I like reading Sam-I-am.*

Whilst many of us (me included) prefer the feel, smell, and general bookness of the printed form, this doesn't mean that other formats aren't 'proper reading'. By being format snobs we are simply excluding others from accessing the joy of books.

E-readers have a number of features that the printed form does not including the ability to change the font and size to suit the reader's needs. The simple ability to change the font from a serif to sans serif could make the world of difference to a student with dyslexia.

For others, being able to swap over to a light font on a dark background in 'night mode' can help reduce eye strain and headaches. If your students complain about headaches when reading, this could well be part of the solution.

Finally, a number of e-readers include the ability to translate text to speech. This allows the student to plug in headphones and read along with the book, improving their literacy in an accessible way.

Audiobooks are not the enemy.

## 76. Have a reading shelf

This applies no matter what subject you teach, and no matter what age they are. Having a small shelf of your own books that you have read, or want to read in your classroom is both a visual clue to who you are, but also provides instant access to reading material for your students.

It also provides a clear message that books don't just belong in a library, but are a part of our everyday lives. As a child, my parents insisted on having no bookshelves in their house as they simply didn't read and considered books to be clutter. In contrast, my bedroom had an entire wall dedicated to my personal 'book stash'. Thankfully, it didn't put me off reading, but I am rather a minority and as an adult am passionate about encouraging easy access to reading material.

My personal classroom book shelf includes a range of books that can be used by my academic classes and my form during DEAR. There are books on there linked to my subject, teaching theory books (allowing students to see that I am still learning too), and a selection of fiction books.

Each book has a label on the front with "this book belongs to Mrs Billinghurst, please return to room 104" just in case a student borrow a book. The fiction books were either donated by friends clearing out their teenager's books, or from my annual charity shop book shopping expedition.

## 77. Add some creative writing

Adding a creative writing task to cross-curricular subjects might not initially fit with your curriculum, but there are a number of scenarios that allow us to implement creative writing tasks outside of the English curriculum.

From a computer science stance, each year has a literacy link. In year 12, as students are introduced to the concept of Finite State Machines (a definitively maths concept), we use them to create a 'choose your own path' story that can be coded. For year 9s, a term of coding is planned around the codebreaking tasks in a secret agent book – each week students are set homework to read the upcoming chapter which gives them the required clues for the next task. This is followed up with a project where students write their own short story with hidden coding clues.

Not only does this provide your subject with a literacy link, but improves their communication levels and allows them to practice essay skills without the inclusion of exam style essay questions.

## 78. Listen to your avid readers

Earlier, I was extolling the value of audiobooks for pronunciation, but not all of our students will use this, and misconceptions will still be with some of them.

One of the downsides of being a bookworm is potentially never hearing the more complex words that you encounter. In fact, some of our students will have a reading age far in excess of their chronological or verbal age. Because of this, they may pronounce newer words phonetically and the pronunciation remains with them until they are corrected – in some cases this will not be until years later unless we *hear them*.[12]

As an avid reader myself, I was terrifically embarrassed to admit that I didn't put the written word 'Lieutenant' and the 'Lef-tenant' word that I heard together until I required closed captions in adulthood. This, as an educated adult was mortifying until I realised that actually it was because much of my vocabulary came from endless reading as a child and teenager.

What I am not saying here is that we should pick up the mispronunciations in front of others, but instead present our key terminology with phonetic pronunciations where possible. Adding phonetic pronunciations to worksheets in a similar style to those seen in a dictionary will help our students of all abilities.

## 79. Investigate the words that you use

If time allows, looking into the historical background of the key words that we use provides students with both an understanding of a key term and a visual reference for remembering.

I am one of a small number of people who bemoans the lack of Latin teaching. Seriously, I'm only 38 – I promise! However, many of the words in use, especially from a maths perspective are formed from Latin. The English language has its roots in so many different invading languages that grasping

---

[2] *See tip 72 – Make Reading Accessible*

the roots of a word can spark a new understanding of where a concept was drawn from.

In my case, I teach students to code using loops – the technical term for this is 'Iteration'.

**itera** (Latin) = **repeat** (English)

**iterate** (Latin) = **again** (English)

So, to iterate is to repeat the code again.

One of my favourite topics for pre-GCSE was an investigation into how language evolved from pictograms in caves right up to saving text and images as digital data. A full 75% of the topic was actually linguistics, but provided glorious context for why data is saved in the way that it is. KS2 & KS3 has historically been a time for laying the foundations of our subjects and with the clearer focus on making KS3 count, topics like this can absolutely be argued as a cornerstone of learning. It was also a key to increasing the percentage of girls becoming interested in STEM as they were given the opportunity to explore the *why* and not just the *how*.

## 80. Embrace comics

This was the result of another Ted Talk. The idea that comics are just for small children has been blown out of the water in recent years, and in fact comics like Marvel and DC were never really intended for children (Deadpool being a prime example here).

I'm not suggesting that you should suddenly become an cartoon artist, but they can certainly be used to unleash the educational potential of students who are opting out, and give us an amazing visual planning tool.

Imagine having a big picture concept that you can then decompose into the ideas and concepts that you want them to learn. Even if the drawn side of the comic is simply a set of stick people or you use an online tool like StoryboardThat, students will take more meaningful clues from the visuals and combine them with your text to create a more impactful message.

Scan the QR code to watch Gene Yuen Lang's Ted Talk.

So, a conversation that will likely be had with many students, becomes a comic strip that can be stuck into their book – you can even create a character that looks a little bit like you to make it more personal.

# You Can Count On Me, I'm A Maths Teacher

Embedding maths into lessons can sometimes feel like a tick box exercise for creating your scheme of work or lesson plan, but rather than all teachers being mathematicians, we are in fact lobbyists. As a society, we have created a maths gremlin that tells people that it's ok to be "bad at maths". In fact, some people wear this as a badge of pride, including parents and teachers.

If this is you, stop it right now (*cue teacher voice*).

This rather bizarre attitude is not unique to maths, but has infected literacy and technology use with me cringing in so many departmental meetings where teachers announce "computers hate me", or "I don't care if the spell it right". This certainly isn't limited to teachers, I've lost count of the number of parents who announce at parents evening that they have no idea about computers beyond sending an email. With their children living in a digital playground, wearing IT illiteracy as a badge of honour is a dangerous path to choose... but that is for a different soapbox.

I have developed a special face for teachers who announce to their class that "I'm rubbish with computers". This is not to say that we shouldn't allow our students to be aware of the areas that we struggle with, but there is a fundamental difference between saying "I have to work hard on understanding maths" and "I can't do maths".

## 81. Divide your class

This Most of us will use group work at some point during the term, if not at least once a week. Even if this is just to work in pairs, rather than identifying a number for each group, ask them to arrange themselves by dividing the class, or as a percentage, or even a fraction.

*Each group should be 1/15 of the class, go!*

Of course, what we meant by that is get into pairs. But this simple adjustment of the way that we ask for things embeds the use of maths into their everyday lives. This in turn helps your maths colleagues to banish the ever dreaded phrase *"when will we ever use this?"*. They'll thank you for it. Repeatedly.

## 82. Create an image

I am the first to remind people that I actually find maths quite tough. This seems very odd for someone who teaches a maths based subject and tutors actual maths. But just because we find something in its traditional form hard, doesn't mean that we can't work hard to be good at it and find strategies that help us.

My personal stumbling block is numeracy rather than application – I can apply decision maths until the cows come home, but ask me to multiply and the numbers start dancing around on the page. YouTube was an absolute blessing for me in this respect, because I was able to relearn the concepts that I missed in school, and never one to be beaten (on anything... ever) I picked up that visual clues made more sense to me.

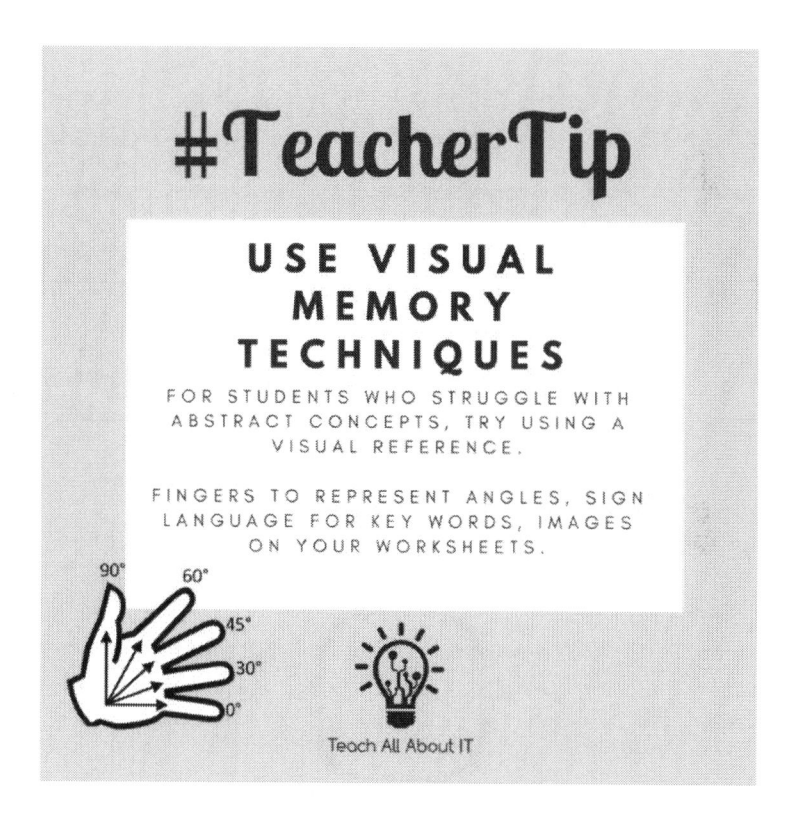

#TeacherTip

**USE VISUAL MEMORY TECHNIQUES**

FOR STUDENTS WHO STRUGGLE WITH ABSTRACT CONCEPTS, TRY USING A VISUAL REFERENCE.

FINGERS TO REPRESENT ANGLES, SIGN LANGUAGE FOR KEY WORDS, IMAGES ON YOUR WORKSHEETS.

Teach All About IT

There has certainly been a step change in maths teaching, and the introduction of regular, low-stakes mental maths quizzes has made a significant difference in the numeracy confidence of an entire generation.

We describe students who don't see concepts in the same way as the general population as *Neurodiverse*. This encompasses a whole host of scenarios from Autism to dyscalculia to dyspraxia. Educational theory has come such a long way over the past few decades with these no longer being considered a barrier to learning, but a brain that is wired differently that requires a different style of teaching.

Before you grab your SEN list, it's worth mentioning that many children with neurodiversity are not diagnosed until much later, possibly even adulthood if they do not fit a set pattern. This is particularly true for girls with autism where difficulties are often masked until puberty. By making learning accessible to a range of learning styles, rather than buying into buzzword pedagogy, we are simply making learning easier to access for everyone.

Using a visual reference can make all the difference to a student – naming their fingers to remember the degree of angles is just one example. Crocodile fingers to represent more than & less than signs (I've lost count of the times that I've said *'use your crocodiles'* in a 6$^{th}$ form programming lesson). Another visual trick is to use the forefinger and thumb to make an 'L' shape – the one on the **L**eft is **L**ess than.

Where students are genuinely struggling to visualise abstract concepts, including basic operations, there is no shame in employing physical items like Lego™ to make the idea more tangible.

For some students, analogies are a good way of making concepts visual:

Want to understand how the code of a webpage works? - *"Your thinking happens inside your head, so the content that the browser needs to know, but not show goes into the head tag"*

Want to grasp the concept of the rule of thirds in design? - *"How do we read a book? Start from the top left and read across – now draw out your lines: if you read the page like a book, where would you start?"*

Thinking outside of the box will not only help you to differentiate for neurodiversity, but will allow students who may not have spoken out to access your topics in a more enjoyable way.

## 83. Make a video

This leads on from my previous tip. Actively learning is generally the most impactful way to study, but as teachers we simply can't be there to repeatedly show the examples again and again for each student. This is where harnessing the video will help students make progress, and will take the pressure off of you in the classroom, especially if you are embedding required maths into another subject.

One thing to note here is that there is no reason to actually appear in the video yourself. The focus of the videos here are generally screen captures or videos of you working through an example of a problem.

To achieve this you can use a whole range of tools, and after some experimenting settle on the one or two that work for you.

$$S = \frac{d}{t}$$

40m in 20s

$$\frac{40}{20} = 2m \text{ per second}$$

If you're using a tablet or laptop with a touchscreen, there are plenty of free apps that will allow you to draw on a digital whiteboard whilst talking and convert this to a video. Alternatively, you can film yourself with a phone or web camera completing a task by hand, then add this to an application such as PowerPoint where you record the narration separately, giving yourself a bit more thinking time.

Once you have created your video, upload it to YouTube (if you don't want it to be publicly viewable, set your upload to 'unlisted'), then either give students a link on their VLE[13], or add a QR code to their worksheet.

## 84. Use statistics

Most subjects require justification of arguments at some point, and when you need to prove a point it's very hard to argue with maths. Except when it is. Statistics are a wonderful tool for considering the use of maths within essays

---

[3] *VLE – Virtual Learning Environment*

or even verbal reasoning, and mainly because they are an example of using maths to prove a point.

My favourite example of this is the 'Ice cream causes shark attacks' argument. Using raw data, it becomes possible to argue that the sale of ice-cream causes shark attacks.

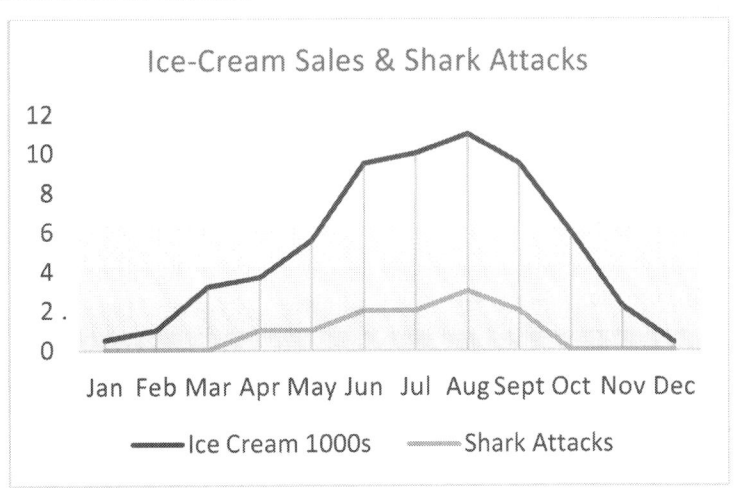

**Ice-Cream Sales & Shark Attacks**

*(Graph showing Ice Cream 1000s and Shark Attacks from Jan to Dec, with values ranging 0–12)*

The statistical evidence clearly points towards this if we just use the graph provided. This allows us to move our students on to consider the difference between correlation and causation – why would ice-cream cause shark attacks? Does this seem right? What other evidence can we look at?

By identifying that we need to look at additional sources and check reliability, you're not just embedding skills in maths but also one of the cornerstones of digital literacy, science, and in fact any subject where facts need to be checked. Check your sources!

A simple graph could lead on to a discussion about WW2 propaganda in History, or the way that statistics are presented in an argument in English, or even how a professional team chooses new players based on their player stats.

## 85. Make it career based

I mentioned above that the phrase that makes most maths teachers' heads spin is "when will we actually use this?". Whilst a pure maths class may well find it difficult to embed constant examples of career links, many other subjects have the potential to provide a tangible benefit to learning specific maths skills.

Simply using the phrase "You've probably come across this in maths" plants the seed of recognition in a student, so when they do use the concept in a more abstract way they have a clear link. Examples for this are often highlighted in science where equations go hand in hand with many concepts. But this is equally true of almost every other subject, especially vocational areas.

In a PSHE lesson about cycle safety, the teacher is talking about riding up a hill and stops. *"By the way, the hill is a 5% incline – just to give us context, how do we work out what the angle is?"*.

In textiles, the teacher is talking about pattern cutting and throws together literacy and maths by reading the Tailor of Gloucester where the tailor is identified as cutting everything on the bias to save fabric, then asking *"How could we use rotation to ensure that the pattern is the right way for all pieces?"*.

None of these examples detract from the content of the lesson, and would have possibly been asked in a different way. It proves the old saying, that we are all maths teachers.

## 86. Explore the ethics of digital art

Exploring the creation of artwork by using a computer algorithm could be explored in a maths, art, design technology, or computer science context.

Tessellations are a specifically mathematical concept, but they are seen in many pieces of art from architecture to Escher.

A graphic design class could investigate how a computer could be programmed to generate a specific tiling pattern that would use rules to ensure that it is aesthetically pleasing and cost effective. This same task could be employed in art to deliberate whether a computer generated design could be considered 'art'.

One of my personal favourites is investigating the relevance of the 'golden ratio' which links the Fibonacci sequence to design concepts, and even crops up in optimum sports placement in field games.

Extending this further, Religious Education students could explore the use of mathematical shapes in a variety of religions. Geometrical patterns can be seen in many different religions and whilst symbols are discussed, this presents an opportunity to identify which symbols are considered geometrical.

## 87. Plan a route

How many times have you relied on your satnav system to find directions for you? Navigation systems use a mathematical algorithm to check time and distance between each place and offer what may be the best route – and herein lies the fascinating part. The shortest path algorithm has actually never been solved! In fact, it can only offer what may be 'good enough'.

Setting students a task to plan a visit using the most efficient use of their time can be achieved without having to explain the detail behind how routes are travelled. For example, if you are planning a school trip with students, set them a task of planning out a route around that will allow them to visit as many areas within a given time.

To take this a step further, once they have plotted a route, identify each place to visit as a 'vertex' and the route to get there as an 'arc' and you've embedded some GCSE maths.

## 88. Calculate time and space

More practical subjects will likely already be embedding maths almost every lesson. The trick is to be able to clearly identify this to the students so that they consistently see small wins in the subjects that they enjoy. There's an excellent reason why many PE teachers also teach maths – and it's usually because they are brilliant at the practical application.

In science lessons, before an experiment takes place asking students "can you estimate how far this will go?" or "can you calculate how long this should take?" embeds the words that they are hearing in maths which are vital to the subject. If it feels weird, an alternative is to point them towards their maths lessons – "you've probably already seen this in maths, and it's really useful here".

When my year 8s are investigating memory for images, we relate this to area & volume in maths:

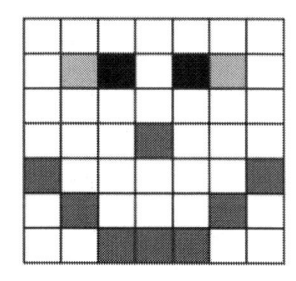

This basic bitmap image is 7 pixels wide & 7 pixels high, meaning we can use the formula for area to calculate the number of pixels:

$w \times h = a$ : $7 \times 7 = 49$

But because there are 4 colours used, each pixel needs 2 binary bits, so there is a depth of 2. Because of this, we can use the same formula as volume:

$w \times h \times d = v$ : $7 \times 7 \times 2 = 98$

Relating this back to something that they have studied in maths makes the concept that we are teaching familiar, and helps our colleagues by answering the question "when am I ever going to use this?".

## 89. Find maths in literature

This is easier for younger years where many books will also have an element of numeracy in them. The Bad-Tempered Ladybird by Eric Carle forms its basis on size comparisons of the animals that it meets, whereas my all time favourite Father Christmas Needs a Wee by Nicholas Allan introduces simple counting techniques by making us all wiggle uncomfortably.

These obvious examples work wonderfully, however there are more discreet ways that maths can sneak into the study of literature.

How many times have you found yourself on the edge of your seat reading a crime novel? (or even watching a crime drama) Solving a difficult case requires proof to be collected and analysed.

*Cue my best Hercule Poirot voice:* Did the prime suspect actually commit the crime? Probably not, and here's why... the mathematical concept of proof by contradiction has been applied! Whilst all the evidence initially points to them, this single piece of evidence proves that it could not have been them.

This same scenario can be applied to a number of the current GCSE English texts, including An Inspector Calls by J.B. Priestly.

## 90. Calculate grades

We all know the feeling of watching students flick straight past the pages of formative feedback on a test to find The Grade. Because of the way that grades are calculated in the UK, this presents all of us with the perfect opportunity to embed some maths into a feedback lesson using a national vs class comparison. This allows the student to achieve two grades – one for a set grade boundary, and another based on their class (this is also really useful for you to identify where your own students are in the national scheme).

At GCSE, the new 9 – 1 grades are worked out using a bell curve method:

**Grade 5** is the median grade (instant maths!)

**Grade 8** is the lowest mark for the top 20%

**Grade 9** is the top 20% of the top 20%

**Grade 6 & 7** are equally spaced in the range between grades 5 & 8

**Grade 1** is the highest mark for the bottom 20%

**Grade 2,3,& 4** are then equally spaced in the range between grades 1 & 5

*Phew!*

Although this may seem complex, working the predicted grades out with a class manually allows them to really consider how dangerous it is to compare themselves to another person's grade as they are actually going to be graded against the other students sitting the exam that particular year.

As a rule, I use a spreadsheet that has been set up with these rules as formulas to calculate the grade boundaries. But in order to create the formulas for that spreadsheet, I needed to understand how they were calculated. Maths creeps in everywhere from checking our change, to calculating more accurate predicted grades.

# The Big Bad I Said No!

Strategies for reducing workload have an awful habit of actually creating more. As a newly appointed learning leader, I developed a spreadsheet for tracking KS3 progress with auto-calculations, colour-coding, and a host of other shiny features that was binned within the year as it created hours of additional work for my colleagues (and me).

I am eternally sorry for jumping in feet first that year.

One thing to bear in mind when looking at workload is that reducing tasks doesn't mean that we are less productive. Instead, what we are removing is the "busy work" that makes us appear productive. As a profession, we have developed an annoying habit of feeling that we need to appear constantly active and progressing. This chapter is here to say to you that less is more, and having a cup of tea and packet of biscuits in front of the TV on a Friday night is not a cardinal sin! (the *whole* packet of biscuits might be a bit much).

So rather than ideas for your students, this final chapter contains ideas to help you to manage the expectations of others and your own.

## 91. Go home

Rude! But actually not what I meant at all.

I had an amazing old school boss some years ago who brought a coffee into my office at 7am and asked me when the last time I'd put my kids to bed was. I had to think! After this, he gave me some particularly sage advice: *teaching is like ivy – it creeps into all the cracks in your life, but if you don't prune it back, it will destroy the foundations. Pruning the ivy doesn't kill it, it makes it healthier.*

Since then, I've made an attempt at sticking to his advice on work / life balance: 49% career, 51% family.

Setting a time to leave is a personal choice for teachers, and we know that taking work home is just an expected part of the job. However it's ok to set boundaries.

One of the strategies that I used in secondary school was to extend my time on site, but take less work home. After school, I remained at my desk until 5pm using that time for marking and planning. Because other people had gone home already, the office was quiet and I achieved more than I would at home where the call of the biscuits was much stronger!

Now, much of my work includes working at home which brings a whole new set of management issues. I am quite literally always at work, so a mental separation needs to be implemented. If you are working from home, either because you are teaching part time, or you are tutoring consider setting specific working times with a clear 'end of the day'. One strategy used widely by tutors is to have a permanent out of office message that reads:

*"Thank you for your email. I am at my desk between x & y, however I may be with another student during these times. Please bear with me, and I will respond to your message within 1 working day."*

In this way, parents have received a response, and your service levels are made abundantly clear.

## 92. Choose your additional duties

As a teacher, you will be expected to undertake a set number of duties such as a breaktime hall duty or supervising a lunch queue. However, beyond this what you choose to undertake is just that, a *choice*.

Having had a heated discussion with a new head of department over who was in charge of Schemes of Work, I am all too aware of how hard it can be to stand your ground, and quite often the volume of additional work that we take on depends on school and departmental morale.

As a rule of thumb, look to how well the foundation work is being completed before agreeing to anything else. Running a club that enthuses students about your subject may sound like a breath of fresh air, but have the assessments been written yet? No, then you know what to do.

A similar rule applies to taking on additional paid duties. Having been up and down the ladder of responsibilities, my advice to any teacher is to look carefully at what will be required versus the compensation offered. It's not always the monetary value, but the time you are given. Is taking on responsibility for two key stages really worth an extra 'free' each week? Or will this encroach into the 49/51 work life balance?

So, what if your decision to apply for a TLR is financial? Movement up the management scale should be because you have a genuine passion for leadership (and if you do, absolute props to you because it's a rough path to follow) – the remuneration per hour is genuinely not going to pay off. There are, however, some tips below that may help.

## 93. Make a list

Lists apply to anyone that is feeling overwhelmed. My desk is scattered with to do lists with ticks showing me clearly when I have achieved what I set out to do.

This visual strategy is great for those of us that work for hours on end and finish the day with a nagging feeling that perhaps we didn't actually achieve much. In fact, you probably did but because, like laundry, the to-do list in education is never ending, it always feels like we could have done a bit more.

If lists aren't quite cutting it for you, another trick that I learnt early on was Time Blocking. This is a strategy that feels very familiar for a teacher because it involves dividing your time up into nice neat little chunks... almost like lessons! On a day where I have planning & preparation time, I set up a list of things I want to work on, and "block" my time.

| 10.00 | 10.15 | 10.30 | 10.45 | 11.00 | 11.15 | 11.30 | 11.45 |
|---|---|---|---|---|---|---|---|
| Make printables | | Respond to Emails | TEA! | Record a video | | Filing | |

To make sure I stick to the timing, I set a timer on my desk which blares out an alarm at the end of my time block. Instead of being focused on completing a potentially never-ending task, I complete a set time working on a task.

When the alarm goes off, it's time to stop the current task and move on. This may create a rising feeling of panic, but because the time blocking is cyclical, you'll come back to complete it with a fresh pair of eyes soon. As counterproductive as it may seem, this little and often approach works wonderfully for creating a sense of achievement and boosting motivation.

Notice also, that breaks are planned in. In this two hour planning & prep time I've included a 15 minute break to make tea & breathe. This is not only ok, but encouraged! If you know that you have time to make a drink & stop in the schedule, you're less likely to procrastinate at the start and just get on with it!

This approach works for so many different things. In fact, I've used it as a revision planner for my students, and a way of getting the house tidy at home. As an anti-procrastination tool, there's nothing better.

Scan the QR code to download my Anti-Procrastination printable and start time-blocking your planning & preparation time. Remember that this is protected planning time for you – if someone encroaches on it, show them that you've your planned time already and ask them to reschedule.

## 94. Take a day off

It seems rather ironic to follow up a pep talk on not procrastinating with a suggestion to stop working, but stick with me here. I'm not suggesting that you should pull a sick day (unless you're actually ill when please do because no-one wants your germs), but I am suggesting that you shouldn't be working 7 days a week.

In a previous job I was invited to a departmental group messenger chat. What was on the surface a way to bond with colleagues and create a sense of community gently morphed into a way for teachers to contact each other outside of working hours and *mention* that they were working. Sunday evening became a competition to see who was working late and eventually I muted the conversation.

**49% work, 51% family**

It is not unreasonable to protect one day each week for yourself, or your family. As a rule, I don't work on a Sunday unless I have a flash of inspiration for writing and we have little else planned. It is ok to fully embrace the hashtag trend of #SelfCareSunday and switch off for a whole day on a regular basis.

In fact, researchers at University College London led by Professor Mika Kivimaki identified that working more than 55 hours per week increased the potential for heart rate irregularities and risk of stroke by five times. This was mainly due to the unhealthy habits that long hours produce. So a regular day of self-care could really have an impact on your health.

## 95. Tidy your desk

As a teenager, my mother used to hover around my bedroom door muttering (loud enough for me to hear) that a *"tidy room creates a tidy mind"*. I hate that she actually had a point.

Worth noting here is that I fully embrace the life of the dusty academic, with piles of books and stationary adorning my desk, alongside a whole host of audio recording equipment. Quite often, I have an array of cups of gently cooling coffee or Early Grey that create a caffeinated version of the scene from Signs... you know the one where the little leaves glasses of water scattered throughout the house. Tidy I am not.

However, in times of great stress one of the quickest ways to feel more in control is to visually organise. Working in a space where you can barely move is not a productive environment and the few minutes you take to throw away the 6 month old sticky notes and gather pens into a single pot, will probably save you hours of losing the papers that you are marking under the rising sea of crap.

If like me, you gaze lovingly at the host of Pintrest™ ideas for a neat classroom, but in fact have the cleaning capability of a toddler perhaps these ideas might help you like they did me:

- Use coloured buckets for pens, scissors, glue
- Assign a 'tidy 10 minutes' to neaten at the end of the day
- File in stages: Box file for incoming, then folders once complete
- Invest in baskets

This final one may require you to purchase the baskets yourself, but having your resources in one box where they can be returned to will really help in your quest to battle the rubbish.

## 96. Write your appraisal

Well this advice just sounds delightful doesn't it? Actually, there's method in my madness here. As teachers, our appraisal paperwork is usually due at the end of September / October when we are swamped with new students and early assessments. Seriously, who wants to write an appraisal then?!

Just like the advice that we give our students, add to the document little and often. Each time you do something great, add in the date and a short note – you don't have to write an essay about it, but enough to prompt you to write more when you have to. This will avoid you sitting with the same look teachers the world over have when they sit in front of a blank self-evaluation wondering "what *did* I do last year?".

A useful tool that I've picked up along the way has been making use of cloud storage. Using a cloud storage app on your phone will often have a tool that allows you to use a photograph to create a document 'scan'. Each time you have something that you want to add, grab your phone and scan it. By September, you'll have evidence galore and won't have to cry into your tea.

## 97. Buy some shoeboxes

When I started my current job, I was greeted by an office with towers of shoeboxes. I could have been forgiven for thinking that the teachers here were trying to build themselves nests for the winter (exam papers would make excellent insulation). In fact, rather than creating insulated hobbit holes, this was actually an ingenious filing system!

Each class was assigned a shoebox into which they put their work. Work could then be transported to the office or home without getting muddled with other classes' work, or damaged.

Whilst this didn't make the process of marking any shorter, it did make identifying and collecting work much easier. More so with the addition of a class list on the top of the boxes, which could be ticked when work was handed in. Students soon got used to this idea and arrived in class expecting to collect their work from the shoebox and dropping in completed work.

Shoeboxes can be collected from friends and family, especially in the summer, when new school shoes are being bought in droves. Alternatively, a set of 10 can be bought online for under £10[14]. If you're feeling creative, you could even cover them with plastic wrapping to give the work an extra layer of protection against the elements.

## 98. Share your resources

Actually no, don't. Or rather, do share them in a way that will benefit you and other teachers. Sharing resources very much depends on how and where you created them. As a rule of thumb, if the resources were created outside of working hours and at home, then they remain your intellectual property. However, it's always worth checking your contract as some schools will have a clause on ownership.

Most teachers will have a wealth of resources that they have created over the years, and probably don't realise that there is another teacher out there who is simply flat out and would pay to be able to download them and save themselves time.

---

[14] My shoeboxes came from: https://amzn.to/2RRdl7z

In 2017, the TES identified that 73% of teachers reported spending their own money on essential items, including resources, due to budgetary limitations. So, much like the 'buy local' approach, an ethical way to make the teacher pound go further is to purchase from colleagues. There are a number of sites that allow you to easily upload resources as digital downloads for other teachers, and for some this equates to a far greater additional income than taking on responsibilities within school. Some teachers, myself included, choose to offer these downloads via their own site due to increasing commission.

## 99. Bring back 'Cake Friday'

In Ye Olde Days of the staffroom, there once was a mythical ceremony at the end of each week. Teachers would gather around in a shared space where no student was to be found, lured by the promise of cake.

As the years went by, managers saw this gathering as a way of adding additional meeting time and eventually, the lure of cake was no longer needed as the meeting was timetabled during break. And thus the cake disappeared with a cost saving and was never seen no more.

What the managers failed to see in this tradition is that is wasn't about sharing pedagogy or discussing progress targets, but a genuine moment of recognition of the hard work that the staff had put in that week. The gift of a cake costing no more than 50p was happily exchanged for hours of unpaid overtime.

This same end of the week recognition is practiced the world over in almost every industry. Offices have 'dress down Friday', or in the case of a local office 'Free Beer Friday' – in each case staff morale is improved through a small, but significant nod to the work they put in.

This is not a difficult tradition to set up within a department, and I wholeheartedly recommend implementing a cake rota. Of course, for the first 2 weeks in September and January when everyone is proclaiming to be healthy because it's the start of the new academic or because New Year's resolutions haven't been discarded like yesterday's pants, you can swap this out for 'Fruit Friday', then happily slip back into old habits. Perhaps bring in some carrot cake to show willing towards vegetables.

## 100. Use the word 'No'

I'm going to leave you with this final tip. Or rather, psychologically give you permission to control your teaching.

Saying "no" is not about being militant, nor awkward. You have chosen to teach because you have a calling – you wouldn't do this unless you loved it. Taking care of yourself by managing your workload is not selfish. You are future-proofing your capacity to continue long-term.

Burning yourself out short term, may provide short term gain for results for one, maybe even two years. But a slow burn will impact and inspire so many more lives.

Saying "no" when you need to will not only reduce your stress levels, but make you a better teacher, and make your students better learners because you'll be present. Hopefully, some of the tips in this book have helped you to say "yes" to making the most out of your classroom and keeping up with the increasing demands of teaching, whilst also being able to say "yes" to retaining a life outside of the classroom.

Whatever stage of your career you are at, whether you're a trainee, an NQT, seasoned teacher, or tutor, I wish you the very best in the future, because you really do know how to Teach All About It.

# References

Srini Pillay, MD. 2018. *The "thinking" benefits of doodling - Harvard Health Blog - Harvard Health Publishing.* [ONLINE] Available at: https://www.health.harvard.edu/blog/the-thinking-benefits-of-doodling-2016121510844.

Nittono, H., Fukushima, M., Yano, A., & Moriya, H. (2012). *The power of kawaii: Viewing cute images promotes a careful behavior and narrows attentional focus.* PloS ONE. *doi: 10.1371/journal.pone.0046362*

Dweck, C., Transcript of "The power of believing that you can improve". *TED: Ideas worth spreading.* [ONLINE] Available at: https://www.ted.com/talks/carol_dweck_the_power_of_believing_that_you_can_improve/transcript?language=en#t-111056

Luen Yang, G., Transcript of "Comics Belong In The Classroom". *TED: Ideas worth spreading.* [ONLINE] Available at: https://www.ted.com/talks/gene_luen_yang_comics_belong_in_the_classroom

Heller-Sahlgren, G., "The achievement-wellbeing trade-off in education". *Centre for Education Economics.* [ONLINE] Available at:

https://www.ifn.se/eng/people/affiliated_researchers/gabriel-sahlgren

Printed in Great Britain
by Amazon